MW00980151

Finding a Job
on the Internet

Other Glossbrenner books

Finding a Job
on the Internet

Alfred & Emily Glossbrenner

McGraw-Hill, Inc.

New York San Francisco Washington, D.C. Auckland Bogotá
Caracas Lisbon London Madrid Mexico City Milan
Montreal New Delhi San Juan Singapore
Sydney Tokyo Toronto

©1995 by **Alfred & Emily Glossbrenner**.
Published by McGraw-Hill, Inc.

Printed in the United States of America. All rights reserved. The publisher takes
no responsibility for the use of any materials or methods described in this book,
nor for the products thereof.

pbk   1 2 3 4 5 6 7 8 9   FGR/FGR   9 9 8 7 6 5
hc   1 2 3 4 5 6 7 8 9   FGR/FGR   9 9 8 7 6 5

Product or brand names used in this book may be trade names or trademarks. Where we believe that
there may be proprietary claims to such trade names or trademarks, the name has been used with an
initial capital or it has been capitalized in the style used by the name claimant. Regardless of the
capitalization used, all such names have been used in an editorial manner without any intent to
convey endorsement of or other affiliation with the name claimant. Neither the author nor the
publisher intends to express any judgment as to the validity or legal status of any such proprietary
claims.

Library of Congress Cataloging-in-Publication Data
Glossbrenner, Alfred.
    Finding a job on the Internet / by Alfred Glossbrenner, Emily
Glossbrenner.
        p. cm.
    Includes index.
    ISBN 0-07-024055-8
    1. Job hunting—Data processing. 2. Résumés (Employment)—Data
processing. 3. Internet (Computer network) I. Glossbrenner,
Emily. II. Title.
HF5382.7.G56 1995
650.14—dc20   94-48313
                                                CIP

Acquisitions editor: Brad E. Schepp
Editorial team: Joanne M. Slike, Executive Editor
               David M. McCandless, Managing Editor
Production team: Katherine G. Brown, Director
                Toya Warner, Computer Artist
                Lisa M. Mellott, Coding
                Susan E. Hansford, Coding
                Wanda S. Ditch, Desktop Operator
                Joann Woy, Indexer
Design team: Jaclyn J. Boone, Designer   0240558
             Katherine Stefanski, Associate Designer WK2

Contents

Part 2
Career explorations

Part 3
Job search tools and techniques

Introduction

Do you have any idea what it's like to hold in your hand a sparkling gem of inestimable value? You want to show it to people. And, once you know that you can reproduce it an infinite number of times, you want to *give* it to people. You want to say, "Here, take this. It will help you." And you can do so freely because you still have your own copy of the jewel. That's the real magic of books. Print as many copies as you like, and the value of any copy is not affected. In this realm, at least, it is the information that matters.

We think that the information you find in *this* book will matter a great deal if you are thinking about changing jobs or are currently embarked on a job search. That's why you are likely to be as amused as we were by the reactions to it.

"We're writing a book about finding a job on the Internet," your co-authors would say. "That's nice, dear," one parent remarked. "I'd think that most people would prefer to work for an established, well-known company. But, as long as that Internet place pays well and offers good benefits—that's what's important to Daddy and me . . ."

Friends and neighbors would offer kind but blank stares. After a polite pause, one would nod and say, "So, how's your garden, then? Any tomatoes yet?"

Another friend, going for her Ph.D. in English literature, frankly admitted that she had never heard of the Internet. (Turns out she was not alone: According to a national survey, only about five percent of the American public has heard of the Internet.)

As it happened, *Moby Dick* was a central work in her dissertation, and when we gave her a copy of the entire novel as a series of text files—obtained for free, via the Net—she was amazed. Imagine being able to search through *every* chapter in this incredible novel for any word of interest, and doing so in *seconds*.

 # Into the flow

But no questions followed. There were no inquiries about, say, the works of Shakespeare or Milton. All of which are equally available on the Net at little or no cost.

So we let it go.

Clearly we live and work in an entirely different world than that of our parents or friends. We send and receive e-mail via the Internet to people in Hong Kong and the Ukraine without a second thought. We are pleasantly surprised—but not amazed—when someone in Argentina sends a message to one of our online addresses saying how much he liked one of our books.

We do our best to reply to each and every message. But this kind of correspondence is not unusual. It is routine. Why would we give it a second thought? Similarly, if there is something we need to know about a company, an individual, an issue, or whatever, we go online and get it.

It's just not a big deal. An agent says, "I'm intrigued by your idea, but I need some sales figures for the work in question." Hey, no problem.

We sign on to a system, do a search of an appropriate database, edit the information we capture, and fire it off to the agent via e-mail.

 # Nothing special

Please believe us—this is nothing special. It's not exotic. It isn't even expensive. The information we eventually fire off to the agent might cost us about $10. And it could lead to a book contract worth many times that amount. Certainly, spending this money is a worthwhile investment.

By now you are wondering, "What does all this have to do with finding a job on the Internet?" The answer is quite simple: The Internet is but one thread in an entire skein of communication and information features available to anyone who has a modem-equipped computer. Whether you are interested in finding a job, finding information about a company that might offer you a job, or finding the sales figures that will satisfy your agent, the answers may very well lie online.

 # Stepping through the chapters

That's why Part 1 of this book is designed to get you up to speed. Here you will learn about the hardware (modems, mainly) and software you need to go online. Then we'll look at the best and most economical ways to get connected to the Internet. Chapter 3 provides an overview of the Internet's major features, and Chapter 4 offers a primer on how to use these features. The last chapter in this part of the book, Chapter 5, clues you in on how to find features dealing with subjects of interest on the Net.

With all of the basics under your belt, Part 2 moves on to career- and job-specific features. Chapter 6 introduces you to non-Internet options, while Chapters 7 through 13 bear down on features you'll find on the Internet. Included are chapters devoted to finding a job in government, academe, and health care, among others.

The major thrust of the information presented in Part 2 is toward *specific* job offerings. The chapters in Part 3 look at the other side of the equation. Here you will learn about preparing your resume, posting it online, and taking action to respond to job offers. You will also learn about tapping into the "hidden job market" by participating in online SIGs and Internet newsgroups.

Chapter 17 shows you how to use the Internet to learn more about professional and trade associations. And Chapter 18 completes the book with some pointed advice on using the information-oriented databases on commercial systems to steal a march on your competition.

Finally, there is an appendix that tells you how to order Glossbrenner's Choice disks. These disks are offered as a convenience to our readers. They contain nothing that you could not get via the Internet yourself, if you had the time and the patience to do so. Indeed, as you will see throughout the book, your co-authors do their best to tell you where to go on the Internet to get each item. But if time is of essence, we are happy to provide you with the files on 3.5-inch disk via Glossbrenner's Choice.

 # Conclusion

This book really is a precious jewel. Your co-authors had nothing to do with this gem's brilliance. We are but simple reporters commissioned to bear witness to the light. We have done our very best to give you what you need to find the job that is right for you.

Yet, in the end, what you make of the resources presented here is entirely up to you. We have no doubt that some options will strike a chord or evoke a resonance, while others will not.

What we do know for sure, however, is that the world of the Internet and e-mail and newsgroups and SIGs and online databases is very much the world of the future. We dearly love our "low-tech" friends, but things really are passing them by.

Your co-authors live and breathe in a world of (mostly) electronic information. And it's no big deal. We don't run, panting, to keep up. Electronic information is our life and our business and our most natural tool.

We know it. We love it. And we are absolutely thrilled to be able to share it with you in a book about finding a job on the Internet. There are so many wonderful things we have to show you that we should simply get to it! Please read on to Chapter 1.

Part 1

Quick-start guides to Internet basics

1

Hardware & software basics

YOU will need four things to tap the Internet and online systems like America Online and CompuServe: a computer, a modem, a telephone outlet, and a communications program. In this chapter, we'll tell you what hardware and software to buy and how to use it to go online.

It's not complicated. It's not expensive. It's even possible that you won't have to buy anything. Your machine may already be equipped with a modem and a comm program. But let's assume that you are starting from ground zero and have nothing but a telephone outlet. Your first step is to buy a computer.

 # Computer brands barely matter

These days, it hardly matters what kind of computer you buy. It used to make a difference whether you bought a Macintosh with its Motorola CPU (Central Processing Unit) or a DOS/Windows machine built around an Intel chip like the 486 or the Pentium.

Today, everything is converging. The latest Macintoshes use the PowerPC chip, a CPU designed and produced by Apple, IBM, and Motorola to try to break Intel's grip on the industry. (Macintosh holds only about 10 percent of the market; everything else belongs to computers built around Intel chips and their clones.) The strategy may just work, for a PowerPC Mac can completely emulate a DOS/Windows machine.

Apple has also finally begun to license its Macintosh operating system software to other computer makers. Although no non-Apple Macintosh computers have appeared at this writing, when they do, it will be possible for an Intel-based computer to completely emulate a Macintosh. And, of course, there will be PowerPC-based machines from IBM and other computer makers.

Computers really have become commodities. So your first consideration these days is likely to be the size and shape of the machine, not its brand. Do you want a notebook-style portable or a desktop system? Obviously, if you can afford it, it would be great to

have both: a lightweight system to travel with and a multimedia-equipped monster with a huge hard drive, a CD-ROM drive, and incredible speakers.

Key points to keep in mind

In general, our advice to anyone interested in buying a computer is this: Get the fastest, most powerful machine you can afford. But that's not the advice we would give to someone who is either unemployed or seriously contemplating a career move. You've got to watch your expenses.

Therefore it's crucial for you to know that even the lowliest, 1981-vintage IBM/PC has all the power you need to tap the online world. In other words, when you are online, the power and speed of your computer are essentially irrelevant. As a job seeker, the place to put your money when it comes to computer equipment is into your printer and your modem. Then use any cash you may have left to spruce up your wardrobe.

When power matters

There *is* one exception to the rule that "power doesn't matter when you're online." That's when you are online with a highly graphical system like the Internet's World Wide Web (WWW). "The Web," as it's often called, is designed to make your computer screen look like a magazine page, complete with different type sizes and type styles and illustrations.

Unfortunately, photos, graphic images, and other illustrations make significant demands on any computer. That's because displaying such *bit-mapped* images requires your computer to individually turn on or off the tiny dots of color that make up your screen. Depending on the size of the image, hundreds of thousands of dots may be involved. So the faster your computer can work, the faster it will be able to handle this chore, and the faster those images will appear.

Of course the bits that make up those images must also be transmitted over the phone line, and this, too, can take a long time. Which is to say, three to five minutes or more *per image*, depending on the size of the image and the speed of your modem. The speed and power of your computer have no effect on this part of the process. It's all up to your modem.

If you're beginning to think you'll have to make a major investment in a powerful computer so that you'll be able to use the World Wide Web, we have some good news. First, online graphics make for some very pretty screens, as we will see, but they are totally unnecessary to an online job search. (Unless, of course, you plan to make your employment decision on the basis of a picture showing a company's headquarters building.)

Second, many Web sites give you the option of turning off graphics and receiving just the text they contain. And most *Web browser* programs (like Mosaic or Netscape Navigator), let you turn off graphics as well. Instead of taking the time to receive and display an image, they give you a generic icon at the place where the image would normally appear. Or you can simply access the Web via Delphi, which, at this writing, automatically turns off graphics. Instead of a picture, you see "[image]" where a picture would be.

All of which is fine. More important, it's fast. And more important still, the power and price of your personal computer have no relevance in this mode since nothing but text is being received and displayed.

⇒ Bottom-line time

The key thing is to put your money where it matters. Thus, we recommend getting a laser printer instead of an ink-jet printer because you will want to be able to produce truly high-quality cover letters and resumes. Similarly, we recommend a 28.8 data/fax modem, not the slower 14.4 variety. A 28.8 modem can send and receive data at double the speed of a 14.4, and that not only saves time, it can save long-distance telephone charges.

Your computer need not cost you a huge amount of money. In early 1995, for example, you could get an IBM-brand 386SX25 machine with a color monitor and a 125-megabyte hard drive for $550. For $1100 you could get an IBM-brand 486SX25 "multimedia PC" with a double-speed CD-ROM drive, a modem, and all kinds of other goodies. Those are desktop systems offered by Computer Palace in New York City. For mail-order information, call 212-629-8977.

At the same time, for $700, you could get a remanufactured Contura Aero 486SX25 notebook-style computer with an 85-megabyte hard drive and a one year Compaq warranty. For information, call Excel Computer & Software in New York at 212-684-6930.

Basic, no frills, Hewlett-Packard (HP)-compatible laser printers were selling at many stores for as little as $400.

Thus, for between $1000 and $1500, you should be able to get a laser printer and a desktop or notebook computer with plenty of power. You may want to spend more for an even faster system, with an even larger and faster hard disk drive, but there's really no need to do so at this point. Don't forget that computers—particularly desktop and tower systems—are usually very easy to upgrade later on. (Tower systems are designed to sit on the floor under or next to your desk.)

 # How to buy a modem

So what about a modem?

A *modem* (short for modulator/demodulator) is the device that converts the electrical impulses computers use internally into sound that can be sent out over the telephone lines. In the simplest terms, a modem lets a computer "talk" on the telephone. As you may know, computers deal exclusively in pulses that physically consist of two different voltage levels. For convenience, everyone calls them on/off *bits* (short for binary digits) and symbolizes them as 1 and 0.

 # Three bit-points

There are three things to remember about computer bits:

> ➤ There is no in-between. Like a light bulb, a bit is either *on* or *off*. There is no dimmer switch to shade things one way or the other.

> ➤ Through the magic of the binary numbering system, you can write any number you like using the 1's and 0's of computer bits. (It just takes an awful lot of them to do it.) If you give *every* letter in the alphabet a number and make sure everyone agrees on these assignments, text can be translated into binary numbers and back again.

> ➤ The bits whizzing around inside your computer consist of very weak voltage pulses. At least they're weak compared to those in the outside world. Before they can be sent into the phone system, they must thus be converted into a more rugged form, in this case *sound*. Which, of course, is what the telephone system was designed for!

 # The question of speed

Modem speeds are measured in *bits per second* (bps). You'll hear the term *baud* used, but it is accurately applied only to 300-baud modems. Stick with bps. Or kbps for *kilobits per second*. Thus 14,400 bps is the same as 14.4 kbps, and 28,800 bps is the same as 28.8 kbps. (The kbps is often left out since, presumably, *everyone* knows that it is implied.)

The official international standard for 28.8 modems was finally approved in June 1994. It's called V.34 and pronounced "vee dot thirty-four." Prior to this, modem companies made modems based on their best guesses as to what the V.34 standard would consist of. They labelled these units *V.Fast*. Do *not* buy a V.Fast modem, should any still be around as you read this. You simply cannot be sure that one maker's V.Fast modem will work at 28.8 with any other maker's model or with models implementing the full V.34 standard.

 # 28.8, data/fax, external

In our opinion, you should buy an external 28.8 kbps data/fax modem. This will cost you about $180. We've had good luck with modems made by Zoom Telephonics. Call the mail-order firm PC/Mac Connection at 800-800-0005 for more information on Zoom and other brands of modems.

It's true that commercial systems like America Online and CompuServe do not yet widely support 28.8 connections. But most independent Internet access providers do, and you will be grateful for your 28.8 capabilities should you ever use your provider to access a World Wide Web site on the Internet. In our opinion, the Web is just barely usable over a 28.8 connection and a complete waste of time at any slower speed.

Since silicon is so cheap, these days most modem makers throw in fax modem capabilities almost as a matter of course. Fax modems are great. They let you fax text and images created with your word processing or graphics software directly from your computer. And since incoming faxes are saved as files on disk, it's easy to forward a fax you have received to someone else.

There are just two drawbacks when compared to a standard fax machine. First, in order to receive a fax, your computer and fax modem must be on, and your fax software (supplied free with your modem) must be loaded. That means your system must be on pretty much all the time. Second, unless you also buy a scanner, you won't be able to fax newspaper clippings or anything else that you did not create on your computer.

Your co-authors operated for many years with just a fax modem, so we know whereof we speak. We are so glad we finally bought a dedicated Panasonic fax machine. And, as a side benefit, whenever we want to "scan" something into our computers, we just use the Panasonic to fax it to our fax modems. (Needless to say, this little trick requires two phone lines.)

 # Internal or external?

There are essentially three modem "profiles"—internal, external, and PCMCIA.

Internal modems are just circuit boards that you plug into a vacant slot on your motherboard (the computer's main circuit board). Once installed, you can plug an internal modem into the phone jack just as if it were a telephone.

External modems are free-standing "boxes" that you connect to the phone line like a phone, and to your computer via the system's *serial* or *RS-232C* port.

PCMCIA modems consist of shirtpocket-sized circuit boards that are protected by a plastic case and equipped to be temporarily plugged into a PCMCIA socket. The letters stand for Personal Computer Memory Card International Association, and while any kind of computer can have a PCMCIA socket, they are most often found on notebooks.

We don't want to make a big deal of this, but we began life online with a 300-baud *acoustic coupler*—rubber cups placed over the ear- and mouthpieces of the telephone handset—and we've used every type of modem since. In our seasoned opinion, you will be much, much happier with an external modem that shows you what's happening by blinking its lights and that you can reach over and shut off when it starts acting up. (If an internal modem starts misbehaving, the only solution is to turn off your computer, wait a minute, and turn it on again. Major inconvenience.)

There's also the fact that you can use an external modem with *any* computer. As long as a computer has a serial port, you can plug in your external modem. You may need to pay attention to the cable, since Macintosh computers connect to external modems with a round, 8-pin DIN plug and DOS machines typically use a DB-25 connector. But such cables sell for less than $6 at stores like Office Depot and Staples.

 # Mind your UART!

In our opinion, the only reason to buy a new internal modem is that your computer was manufactured prior to 1992. Such machines typically do not have the ability to use modems faster than 9600 bps. If you have such a machine, installing an internal card-mounted 28.8 kbps modem corrects the problem. Alternatively, you can install a new serial card for about $40 and plug a 28.8 external modem into *it*. (We've had good luck with the high-speed serial cards sold at Egghead Software.)

The key term to watch for is "16550A UART." The UART is the Universal Asynchronous Receiver/Transmitter chip that is the heart of your serial communications port.

If you're in doubt about what you've got, ask your favorite computer guru. Or run a program like UARTID.EXE, which will check your serial communications ports and report the results. If it finds a 16550A UART chip, then you can indeed operate at 14.4 or 28.8 with the appropriate external modem. If it doesn't, then you will have to either replace the serial port connection or go with an internal modem.

UARTID.EXE is available on the Glossbrenner's Choice disk Utilities 9, System Configuration Tools. (See the appendix of this book for ordering information.)

What about PCMCIA?

Most notebook and other portable computers come with a serial port, so you can plug in a conventional external modem if you want to. You would not want to lug such a unit around, however. Alternatively, you might be able to equip your notebook with an internal modem. No muss, no fuss, just plug in the phone line whenever you want to communicate. It's neat, but then you are always carrying your modem with you as part of your computer.

The PCMCIA modem-on-a-card solution solves both problems. It's light, self-contained, and detachable. You don't have to take the modem with you unless you want to. All of which is to the good.

The downside is the expense. PCMCIA modems tend to cost more than comparable external or internal models. And there's the convenience factor. An internal modem may add a bit of weight to your system, but it eliminates the need to think ahead. Who knows where you'll be before day's end or how many times you will want to be able to go online? If you've got an internal modem, you may not even have to worry about bringing along a phone cord, since you can simply unplug a telephone and plug in your computer at many locations.

Two other considerations. First, you may have to pay a bit more for a notebook equipped with a PCMCIA socket. Second, battery life. Internal modems and PCMCIA modems alike draw the power they need from your computer. If the computer is plugged into an electrical outlet, no problem. Otherwise, they will both drain your battery.

 # Moving on to software

Communications software is so fundamentally simple that comm programs have been forced to become complex.

Yes, that sounds like a Zen koan or other concept for long contemplation. But it's true. From a programming standpoint, basic computer communications is very simple. It's a matter of initializing the UART/comm port and directing everything you type to both the screen and to that port. On the receiving end, it's a matter of directing everything that comes in the UART/comm port to the screen, or, optionally, to the printer or a disk file.

End of story.

No wonder the smallest communications program in the world is only six lines of BASIC programming. That's why commercial comm programs *must* be complex. That's why they *must* offer dozens of features you will never, ever use. How else can their creators justify charging $40 to $100 for them?

 # Free & shareware programs

These days, communications software is almost a non-issue. America Online (AOL), CompuServe, and Prodigy, the leading commercial online systems, all but give their access software away. Actually, AOL and Prodigy have to do this since the only way to access their systems is with their in-house software. That's because Prodigy and AOL get around the need to transmit graphics over the phone lines by storing basic images on your disk. Any basic AOL or Prodigy graphic image can then be displayed in response to a very short command sent from the host system. CompuServe (and Delphi and GEnie and all bulletin board systems) can be accessed with virtually any comm program.

If you are a Windows 3.1 user, you will find that you've got a basic comm program in the application called Terminal. (Click on the Main program group and then on the Terminal icon.) If you are a Macintosh user with System 7 Pro, see your documentation for instructions on using the PowerTalk communications module that is part of that program.

Alternatively, if you are using any of the leading "works" packages—ClarisWorks, GreatWorks, Microsoft Works, or WordPerfect Works—you will find that you already have a comm program as well. WordPerfect Works for DOS machines also includes a comm program module.

If absolutely *none* of this applies to you, don't worry. You are still in luck, because there are wonderful public domain and shareware comm programs available for *every* kind of machine. *Public domain* programs are yours to do with what you wish. *Shareware programs* amount to "software on the honor system." Which is to say, you are on your honor to send the program creator the requested registration fee if you like and regularly use the product. (Such fees are typically

only about $25 to $40, and paying them often gives you access to help and support directly from the program's creator.)

The shareware comm program we like best for DOS machines is Qmodem from Mustang Software. For Windows, our current favorite is a program called CommWin. (Both are available from Glossbrenner's Choice.) If you're a Macintosh user, call Educorp, one of the leading distributors of Mac shareware, and request a free catalogue. The number is 800-843-9497. There is simply no need to pay a lot of money for a first-class comm program.

It's also worth noting that Internet access providers typically give you, free of charge, either their own proprietary software—like Netcom's NetCruiser or The Pipeline's Internaut program—or they give you shareware or public domain programs like the Internet electronic mail (e-mail) program Eudora and the Web browser Netscape Navigator (by the creators of the original Mosaic program).

 # Basic comm program functions

Again, getting the communications software you need just isn't an issue. Most modems, in fact, arrive with "lite" versions of commercial data and fax communications software. Learning to *use* a given comm program, however, is another matter.

Personal computers are the most powerful, complex devices created by mankind in the 10,000 years of its existence. Yet most people refuse to spend even a few minutes with an instruction manual that tells them how to use these machines. We agree that most hardware and software manuals are terribly written—if they were well done, there would be little need for most computer books—but why would anyone expect this most complex piece of equipment to be easier to use than a microwave oven?

As a prospective Internet and online services user, you must simply face that fact that you are going to have to "learn to ride the bicycle" before you can expect to get anywhere. The bad news is that many

different makes and models of "bicycles" are available. The good news is that they all perform the same basic functions.

Once you know what the functions are, it's not too difficult to zero in on them and on the commands your particular software requires to perform them. It is the general functions that we will present here.

Basic basics

At the most fundamental level, a comm program opens a channel between your keyboard and your modem, allowing you to "talk" to the modem directly when you are in *terminal mode*. Once you are in terminal mode, you can key in AT or at and the modem should respond by displaying "Okay" or "OK" on your screen. (The AT command essentially says "Attention, modem.")

If you have a modem connected to your machine and you do the AT bit and get no response, check each of the following, if applicable:

➢ Your cable connections. Is everything plugged in firm and secure?

➢ Your power connections, if you're using an external modem.

➢ The COM port address. DOS/Windows machines can support four or more communications ports—typically COM1 through COM4. If your modem does not appear to work, make sure that your communications software is set to "talk" to the port the modem is connected to.

If you are a new user, set your comm software to talk to COM1 through COM4 in turn. After changing each setting, get into terminal mode and key in AT. If you get no response, tell the comm software to address the next higher COM port. If you try all four and still have no "Okay," call in a computer guru.

Or, if you are not a comm novice, check the modem or software manual for references to "jumpers" or DIP (dual inline package) switches. The key point is that the port your comm software addresses must be the same port to which your modem is attached.

 # The tools you've got to work with

The most crucial point when communicating with any remote system is that *your* settings match the settings of the remote system. There are just two general settings: 7/E/1 and 8/N/1. Translated, that means "7 data bits, Even parity, and 1 stop bit" and "8 data bits, No parity, and 1 stop bit."

You don't need to worry about what the settings mean. All that matters is that your settings match the settings of the system you're calling. Start with 7/E/1 and if it does not work, try 8/N/1. The Help file or printed manuals that came with your software will tell you how to control these settings.

Now let's take a moment to identify the most important features offered by any comm program.

✳ Capture buffer

In computer talk, a *buffer* is simply an area of memory set aside to serve as a temporary holding tank. When the tank fills up with incoming text, the software dumps it to disk, using a filename you have previously specified. If you don't open your capture buffer or otherwise tell your comm program to "log to disk," all incoming text will simply scroll off the screen, never to be seen again.

✳ Dialing directory or phone book

Most comm programs let you record frequently dialed numbers in a *phone book* or *dialing directory*. That means you can use a key combination like Alt-D and be presented with a list of numbers. Pick a menu item off the list, and the program will automatically dial the number. (You key in a single menu item number, and the software does the rest.)

✳ Scripts

Many comm programs today let you prepare *scripts* that tell them to dial a number, wait for a particular response, and, only when they see such a response, issue some command. With the right comm program

and the right script, you could issue a single keyboard command and have the software dial up, say, CompuServe, download any mail messages in your mailbox, and sign off. And you could arrange to have this done at any hour of the day or night—automatically.

✳ Upload/download protocols

A *protocol* is nothing more than an agreement between two machines on how they will handle the delicate task of transferring an error-free copy of a file from one system to another. A number of protocols—often called *error-checking protocols*—exist. Among them, XMODEM is the lowest common denominator, while ZMODEM is unquestionably the best. In between are Kermit, YMODEM, and XMODEM 1K.

✳ Terminal emulation

To this day, the vast majority of online, personal computer communications is based on the old mainframe-and-terminal model. That model is simple to understand: You've got a big, expensive, powerful mainframe computer located in a climate- controlled "glass house" somewhere, and you've got any number of dumb terminals scattered about.

The dumb terminals consist largely of a keyboard and a screen and have very little processing power of their own. But each does have certain characteristics. The most common set of characteristics are those embodied by the DEC VT-100 model terminal. Thus, many of the sites you log into on the Internet will expect you to "be" a VT-100. Your comm software can almost certainly produce a convincing illusion, but you've got to tell it to do so.

If you plan to access the Internet often, make "VT-100 emulation" the default setting for your comm program. This will not interfere with most of your other online activities, but it will simplify things greatly when you use an Internet feature called Telnet to connect with some location on the Net.

 # Conclusion

There are two main things to remember about comm programs and file transfers. First, for one computer of any sort to talk to another, both have got to agree on their communications settings. If you're set for 7/E/1 and the system you're calling is expecting 8/N/1, you will see garbage characters on your screen. Solution: Change your settings to 8/N/1 and call back. Or vice versa if you called in settings for 8/N/1 and the host was expecting 7/E/1.

Second is the difference between *ASCII text files* and *binary files*. The American Standard Code for Information Interchange or ASCII (pronounced "askey") is the internationally agreed-upon code that assigns a specific number to each upper- and lowercase letter of the alphabet. An ASCII file is a text file. And text files need no special treatment when being transferred from one spot to another.

Why? Because if one or more text characters are garbled in transmission, the entire file is not ruined. You can puzzle out the correct letters or call the sender and ask for clarification. But if even a single byte in a program or archive file is corrupted, the entire file may be useless. That's why an error-checking protocol like ZMODEM must be used to guarantee that a perfect copy of the file arrives on your disk. Just remember that *both* sides of a connection must support the same protocol if you want to be able to use it.

Getting connected

CHAPTER 2

O NCE you've got your computer, modem, and communications software up and running, the next thing to do is to get connected to the Internet. In this chapter, we'll show you how to do exactly that. And we will offer our strong advice on which options you should take.

⇨ Three kinds of connections

In general, there are three main ways one can tap into the Internet:

> ➤ A dedicated, hard-wired, high-speed connection. This is the kind of connection you will find at most college and university computer centers and at large companies.

> ➤ A SLIP/PPP connection. These are the kinds of connections offered by companies called *Internet access providers*. Prices vary widely, but the cost is typically $20 a month for about 10 hours of usage, with additional hours billed at about $2.00 an hour.

> ➤ A dial-up connection. These are the kinds of connections offered by systems like America Online, CompuServe, Delphi, GEnie, Prodigy, and some bulletin board systems (BBSs).

⇨ T1 & T3 connections

Dedicated connections use what are called *T1* or *T3 carrier lines*. Such phone lines typically cost thousands of dollars to install and involve charges of hundreds to thousands of dollars a month. Which is why you will only find such connections at universities and business sites.

The main advantage of a T1 or T3 connection is speed. A T1 line operates at 1.544 megabits (million bits) per second, and a T3 line operates at 44.736 megabits per second. For the sake of comparison, a 28.8 kbps modem operates at 0.0288 megabits per second. So a T1 line is 54 times faster than your modem, while a T3 line is 1553 times faster!

At speeds like these, the files you request from a distant site using the Internet's File Transfer Protocol feature (FTP) arrive almost instantaneously. And the World Wide Web, with all its fonts and graphic images, is finally truly usable.

 # The SLIP/PPP option

A SLIP or PPP connection offers you all the features of a dedicated line, without the speed and without the expense. The acronyms stand for Serial Line Internet Protocol and Point-to-Point-Protocol. All you really need to know, however, is that a PPP connection is the faster, more advanced option.

As we said earlier, SLIP/PPP connections are offered by Internet access providers—companies that have brought in a T1 or T3 line and arranged to sell you access to it. When you call one of these locations, you are connected to the provider's computer which, in turn, is connected to the Internet. But, while information may travel to your provider's computer at T1 or T3 speeds, it travels to you over ordinary telephone lines at your modem's top speed.

There are two main advantages to a SLIP/PPP connection. First, you will have full access to all of the Internet's many features. This is significant because even at this writing, commercial systems like America Online and Prodigy don't provide access to *all* Internet features.

Second, there's the matter of your Internet e-mail address. If you use a commercial online system to send and receive Internet electronic mail, the name of that system will be a part of your address: **JSmith@AOL.com**, **BJones@CompuServe.com**, and so on.

If you use a SLIP/PPP connection, in contrast, you will almost certainly have the option of establishing your own *domain name*. Under the Internet way of doing things, the part of an electronic mail address that ends in ".com," ".org," ".edu," and so on is the domain name. You can tell from this part of a person's Internet address what type of organization they are associated with (.com for commercial business, .org for nonprofit organization, .edu for colleges and universities, etc.).

It may or may not be important to you, but if you want to have an Internet address like **JSmith@SmithInc.com** or **BJones@BJConsult.com**, you will need to get an account with an access provider who can give you a SLIP/PPP connection to the Internet. That provider may also charge you a small fee for doing the electronic paperwork required for you to create your own domain name.

 # Dial-up connections

The quickest, easiest, and possibly least expensive way to get onto the Internet is to do so with a *dial-up* connection. The terminology is anything but precise.

The problem is that the Internet world hasn't come up with a term that distinguishes between a dial-up SLIP/PPP connection and a dial-up connection to Delphi or America Online. Through custom, however, the term "dial-up Internet connection" is usually applied only to connections made through systems like GEnie, Prodigy, and the rest, or through a bulletin board system (BBS).

There are five well-established dial-up systems to choose from: America Online (AOL), CompuServe Information Service (CIS), Delphi, GEnie (General Electric Network for Information Exchange), and Prodigy. All of them have Customer Service numbers you can call when you need help, and all of them offer online assistance in the form of clubs, special interest groups (SIGs), RoundTables, or forums dedicated to the Internet.

 # Easy to subscribe

With literally millions of people using these systems every day, all you have to do is "post" your question in one of these Internet-oriented groups, and there's an excellent chance of getting a response in less than 24 hours.

It's easy to subscribe to a dial-up system. If you've got a comm program and are reasonably comfortable using it, all you need to do to instantly get an account on CompuServe, Delphi, or GEnie is to

call the voice-line numbers given later in this chapter and ask how to sign up online.

Since Prodigy and AOL require you to use their own software, you may have to wait for it to arrive in the mail. Alternatively, you may be able to find "start-up kits" for these and other systems at your local bookstore or computer store. A McGraw-Hill book called *The On-Line Job Search Companion* by James C. Gonyea includes the Windows version of AOL's software along with their standard "10 free hours" introductory offer. (We'll have much more to say about Mr. Gonyea and his AOL Career Center in Chapter 7.)

The costs of using a dial-up system are relatively low, and getting lower as competition heats up. Most systems have a subscription fee of about $10 a month, in return for which they give you either a certain number of free hours or unlimited access to a basic package of services. Additional hours or access to "premium" features is billed at a rate of between $1.80 and $4.80 an hour (usually rounded to the nearest minute), depending on the system.

Also, as long as you don't live too far from a major city or town, there's no need to worry about long-distance telephone charges. Thanks to *packet-switching networks* operated by companies like SprintNet and Xstream (formerly Tymnet), as well as the networks operated by CompuServe and GEnie, you can usually sign on by making a local call to a nearby *network node*. The subscription information for all systems will tell you exactly what to do to find the phone number of your nearest node.

Good news/bad news

That's the good news. The bad news is that only Delphi gives you *full* access to all Internet features. America Online is close, however. At this writing, the only thing AOL is missing is access to the World Wide Web, and it has promised to provide that feature soon. All five systems let you send and receive Internet e-mail. But the other Internet offerings on CompuServe, GEnie, and Prodigy are so limited that we simply cannot recommend them at this time. They have lots of other features of interest to anyone seeking a job, however, so don't rule them out completely.

For more information . . .

As the authors of The Little Online Book *from Peachpit Press, you can well imagine that we would recommend that title to anyone who wants to know more about Prodigy and CompuServe and everything else in the "electronic universe." And we do. Not only does the book give you the kind of hands-on information you need to pick and use a system, it's got lots of truly funny, gentle cartoons by a genius named John Grimes.*

However, you really don't need that book right now. All you have to do at this point is contact each of the systems at the numbers given below and ask for an information packet:

America Online (AOL)	*800-827-6364*
CompuServe Information Service (CIS)	*800-524-3388 or 800-848-8199*
Delphi Internet Services, Inc.	*800-695-4005*
GEnie	*800-638-9636*
Prodigy	*800-776-3449*

 # What's best for you?

So what should you do? If you are currently employed and are allowed to access the Internet through your company's network connection, well and good. It's not as convenient as doing so from home, but it's bound to be the fastest connection around.

On the other hand, if you're interested in finding a company that can provide you with a SLIP or PPP connection, you may want to consult the POCIA (Providers of Commercial Internet Access) list maintained by the Celestin Company. This list gives you the name, voice phone, and e-mail address of hundreds of access providers in the U.S. and around the world. U.S. providers are organized by area code for easy reference.

You'll find the latest copy of the POCIA list on the Glossbrenner's Choice disk, Internet 9, Making Money on the Internet. (The well-known PDIAL list we used to recommend appears to be dead, since it has not been updated in over a year.)

If you know the Internet, you can get the POCIA list by FTP-ing to **ftp.teleport.com** and looking in the vendors/cci/pocia directory for the file called pocia.txt. Or you can send a blank e-mail message to **cci@olympus.net**.

Also, if you are currently using a system that offers Internet *newsgroups* (or *Usenet newsgroups*), take a look at the group called **alt.internet.access.wanted**. There you will find lots of tips, advice, and requests from Internet users around the world.

Leading World Wide Web browser programs

When Microsoft finally ships the next version of Windows—the one formerly code-named Chicago and now called Windows 95—users will find that Internet access is built into the program. It will be interesting to see what Microsoft comes up with. In the meantime, you may want to consider an Internet access/World Wide Web browser from one of the following companies. All of these programs are for SLIP/PPP connections.

Company	Product	Price	Contact
NCSA Champaign, IL	Mosaic	Freeware	217-244-0072 ftp.ncsa.uiuc.edu
Netcom, Inc. San Jose, CA	NetCruiser	Free with subscription	800-353-6600
Netscape Communications Corp. Mountain View, CA	Netscape Navigator	$39 (includes a manual)	415-254-1900 info@mcom.com http://home.mcom.com
O'Reilly & Assoc. Sebastopol, CA	The Mosaic Handbook (includes Enhanced Mosaic software)	$29.95	800-998-9938
The Pipeline New York, NY	Internaut	Free with subscription	212-267-3636 info@pipeline.com
Spyglass, Inc. Naperville, IL	Enhanced Mosaic	$29.95	708-505-1010 info@spyglass.com http://www.spyglass.com
Spry, Inc. Seattle, WA	Air Mosaic and Internet-in-a-Box	$199/$149	800-777-9638 http://www.spry.com

 # SLIP/PPP problems?

All of the World Wide Web illustrations in this book arrived at our computers via a SLIP/PPP connection using Netscape Navigator Web browser software. At this writing, if you want to see the same kind of thing on your screen, you will definitely need a SLIP/PPP connection and Netscape Navigator, Netcom's NetCruiser, The Pipeline's Internaut, or some other graphical interface.

But there are other considerations. There certainly are many excellent SLIP/PPP access providers. Many have local access points in multiple states. And most automatically supply you with the software you will need to use their service.

In selecting a SLIP/PPP provider, be sure to ask about the company's *level of connectivity*. The best providers are those locally- or regionally-based companies that have multiple T1 lines connecting them to the Net.

Companies offering national access, like Netcom, The Pipeline, PSI, and others can be at a disadvantage here. They may have local access numbers in a city near you, which eliminates the need to make a long-distance phone call. But, once you call these numbers, you are typically patched through to the company's Internet access site— which may be thousands of miles away.

As we have said, physical distance doesn't matter once you are on the Internet; but it *does* matter as you are being patched through.

Keep this in mind as well: So many people have leaped into this business that customer service and support can be spotty. You may actually be better off accessing the Net through one of the less expensive dial-up systems, at least until you land that dream job.

It is indeed true that the SLIP/PPP approach offers you 28.8 kbps access and full, graphical access to the World Wide Web. But as we noted in Chapter 1, although many job-related features have Web sites, Web graphics have little to do with a job search.

Dial-up systems like CompuServe offer 14.4 access in some selected cities, but no one yet offers 28.8 connections. And, in any case, the kinds of things you are likely to be doing on the Net as part of a job search probably will not involve downloading lots of very large files.

 # America Online, Delphi, or both?

Everything is subject to change. But if you are just starting out, you are likely to be best off tapping the Internet through either America Online or Delphi. Unless you absolutely must have World Wide Web graphics, there is no compelling reason for a *newbie* (a new user) to start with a SLIP/PPP connection. (And, as noted elsewhere, America Online has promised to provide full graphical Web access in the near future.) Still, whether it's AOL or Delphi, there are pluses and minuses to be considered for both.

 ## AOL: Pros & cons

An AOL subscription is $9.95 per month and includes five free hours on the system, at any time of day or night. Additional connect time is billed at a rate of $2.95 per hour. AOL is also the prettiest system, offering a visually pleasing interface that's both fun and easy to use. (See Fig. 2-1.)

The company has really done things right in implementing its Internet Center features. You have to have used Gopher and FTP on other systems, including SLIP/PPP connections, to appreciate how incredibly easy America Online makes things. (As you will see in Chapter 3, Gopher is a menu-driven Internet feature designed to make the Net much easier to use.)

The company has done an absolutely splendid job that has set the standard for the entire industry of consumer-oriented online systems. Equally important, as you will see in Chapter 6, AOL offers the most extensive non-Internet job-search-related features available anywhere.

Figure 2-1

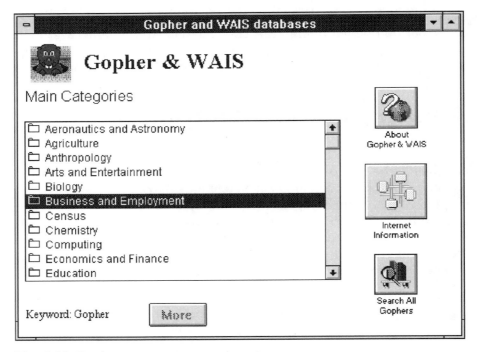

The AOL Gopher menu.

The only drawback to AOL is that there have been times in the past
when it has been impossible to get onto the system due to limited
capacity. Considering that AOL added over 750,000 users between
July 1993 and August 1994, it would have been miraculous if it
hadn't had such problems. The system now boasts over 1.5 million
subscribers, and, as far as we can tell, capacity problems are a thing
of the past, at least during normal business hours.

Delphi, the ugly duckling

Delphi, in contrast, is second only to GEnie in offering a truly ugly
user interface. A graphical package has been promised, but in the
meantime, everything is text. (As we said in Chapter 1, when you use
Delphi to access a World Wide Web site, you will see "[image]" in
place of the graphic that would appear if you were using Mosaic or
some other Web browser via a SLIP/PPP connection.)

But that means that Delphi is fast! As for ease of use, if you can key in an option from a menu, you can use Delphi as easily as any other system. After all, what is a row of mouse-clickable icons if not a "menu" of available options? And text-based menus are so much easier to decipher.

Delphi's simple, text-based interface means that you can use the most basic communications program to raid the Internet and be in and out and offline before someone else can even *reach* the Internet area on America Online. It's also much easier to record your session as a capture file on disk, something that must be done piecemeal on AOL, with lot's of clicking and selecting and filename specifying. With Delphi, you simply open your comm program's capture buffer as soon as you sign on, specify one filename, and record *everything* to disk.

The main drawback to Delphi is cost. A Delphi subscription with full Internet access is $13 a month. That gives you four free hours, with additional time billed at a rate of $4.00 an hour. If you're willing to commit to $23.00 a month, however, you'll get 20 free hours, with extra time being billed at $1.80 an hour.

None of which sounds too bad. Trouble is, the free hours are really only "free" if you use the system during non-prime-time: 6:00 P.M. to 6:00 A.M. on weekdays and all day on weekends and holidays. If you need to use Delphi during prime time, you'll pay a surcharge of $9.00 per hour for using Xstream or SprintNet.

Bulletin board systems, the Internet, & jobs

Bulletin board systems (BBSs) are also a crucial part of the online world. Some of them offer Internet access, and many more of them offer points of contact and valuable career-specific information. We'll tell you about these aspects directly, but first it is important to make the term clear.

Prodigy calls its online special interest groups "bulletin boards," and the laymen's press has often been guilty of calling entire systems like AOL and CompuServe "bulletin boards."

But in the online community, *bulletin board* has always meant a *bulletin board system* or BBS. And that has generally been defined as some guy or gal's computer sitting at home running special BBS software. The BBS owner is called the *sysop* ("sis-op"), short for system operator, and the software allows the sysop's computer to answer modem calls and log people on just as if they were connecting to CompuServe or some other commercial online system.

Indeed, although the original BBSs were established as mere hobbies, these days, BBSs have become so sophisticated that it can be difficult to tell one from a commercial online system. Years ago, the typical board had only one phone line.

The biggest board in the world

That certainly was the case when Bob and Tracey Mahoney started Exec-PC on Thanksgiving Day, 1983. Today, Exec-PC is the largest board in the world, boasting nearly 300 incoming lines, each attached to its own PC and modem. It has logged over 9 million calls since 1983 and is a very profitable enterprise.

Exec-PC charges $25 for a three-month subscription or $75 for a one-year subscription. These fees include five hours of full-featured Internet access per week. Other, expanded, Internet time options are available as well. Plus, you can dial into Exec-PC using CompuServe's packet-switching network, so you probably won't have to place a long distance call. (For more information on Exec-PC, call 800-393-2721.)

According to our friend Jack Rickard, editor and publisher of *Boardwatch Magazine*, there are perhaps 40,000 BBSs in the United States today. Some, like Exec-PC, are massive, general interest boards. But many others are devoted to some special subject or area.

A numbers game

Among the areas of focus are *careers* and *job listings*, to be sure.
But there are also boards devoted to just about any subject, business,
industry, or profession you can imagine. Engineering, medicine, small
business, accounting, construction, data processing, and on and on.
The federal government and many states also operate BBSs with the
sole purpose of posting job openings.

There's an easy way to generate a list of just those boards that deal
with careers and jobs, or just those boards devoted to, say, music
education. But before we tell you about it, we must bring out the old
wet blanket.

Bulletin boards are wonderful creations, and we've been alerting
people to their potential for over a decade. But job seeking is often a
numbers game, and most boards simply don't have the numbers. Be
generous: assume that the typical jobs-oriented BBS has five phone
lines and that it is available 24 hours a day. Assume that the typical
online session lasts half an hour. That's a maximum of 240 online
sessions per day.

But how many corporate recruiters and personnel officers are likely
to be online with that BBS at 3:00 A.M.? Indeed, how many of the
people who are in a position to hire you are likely to take the time
and trouble to dial up that board at all?

Painful as it is to say, unless you've got some *very* unique skill,
training, or job experience, it is highly unlikely that any employer is
going to come looking for you. And no one is likely to spend the time
and effort needed to track down a BBS and sign on to it every third
day on the off chance that you have uploaded your resume.

The best use of BBSs

The best use of bulletin boards, then, is not for posting resumes.
(Although we encourage you to do so as long as you don't have to
pay for the privilege.) No, the best use of BBSs is to learn about a

local area: What's going on in Columbus, Ohio? Who's hiring? What are they looking for? And what about the local schools, taxes, and cost of living?

Or you can use BBSs to chat and exchange ideas and possible job leads with others in your profession or industry. You know people and you hear things. And your fellow BBS users know people, and *they* hear things. At this level, bulletin boards combine human and computer "networking" into an awesome entity that could just end up leading you to your job of choice.

In short, BBSs can be very worthwhile tools in your job search. But in our opinion, they are a secondary tool. For a given amount of effort, you can reach and tap the wisdom of far more people using the Internet and commercial online systems like AOL and CompuServe than will ever be possible using the typical bulletin board system.

 # Finding the right BBS

Lots of magazines offer lists of bulletin board systems and their access numbers. But let's cut to the chase. If you were our brother or sister, we would suggest taking two steps. First, go to your local Waldenbooks or Dalton's or newsstand and get a copy of *Boardwatch Magazine*. There are pretenders to the throne, but this is quite simply *the* magazine for BBS sysops and users. If you can't find the magazine, call 800-933-6038 for more information.

Second, and even more important, is to buy two consecutive issues of *Computer Shopper* magazine. This magazine has long published a very current list of BBS numbers. But the list has grown so long that in early 1994, it began publishing only half of the list in each issue. That's why you will need the lists published in two consecutive months.

Call your library

Computer Shopper BBS listings include descriptions of each board's purpose or focus, so it's relatively easy to single out the boards of

greatest interest. But it's even easier still if you can contrive to get the *Computer Shopper* list in electronic form.

Call your local library or libraries and ask to speak to the reference librarian. Ask that person whether the library offers the Ziff-Davis *Computer Select* CD-ROM, or any other Ziff-Davis CD-ROM product. If it does, you will be able to go to that library and use the product to search *Computer Shopper* for the bulletin boards that are devoted to some specific topic, whether it's engineering or jobs or careers.

The *Computer Shopper* BBS list online

If your local libraries cannot help, your next best bet is the Ziff-Davis Computer Database Plus *on CompuServe. Key in* go compdb *and specify "Computer Shopper" as the publication you want to search. Narrow the results by publication date ("January 1995," for example). Then narrow the results once again by keyword, specifying "bulletin boards."*

Bulletin boards get so much coverage in Computer Shopper, *including a regular column called "Treading the Boards," that you need to narrow the search this way to avoid getting a list of hundreds of articles. This technique will produce a list of but one or two:*

```
Searching..Computer Database Plus Search Summary
Search Method    Search Expression              Articles
Publications     "computer shopper"               6099
Dates            january 1995                      702
Key Words        bulletin boards                   169

Articles that match ALL the search terms above:      1
NEXT ACTION

  1 Display Article Selection Menu
  2 Match Only Full-text Articles
  3 Narrow the Search
  4 Undo Last Search Step
  5 Start a New Search
  6 Display Charge Summary

Enter choice (? for help) ! 1
Computer Database Plus                   Article Selection Menu

  1  Bulletin boards., Computer Shopper, Jan 1995 v15 n1 p633(29).
     Reference # A15944603   Text: Yes (49408 words)   Abstract: No
```

This will give you half the list. To get the full list, you would have to repeat the procedure, specifying "December 1994," the previous month. By the time you have both halves of the BBS list, you will have spent about $6.00. But you will find that this is worth the money, since you will be able to use your word processing software or some other program to search the lists for the BBSs most likely to be of interest. This is much better than pouring over the printed pages of Computer Shopper.

3
Internet basics

CHAPTER 3

WITH the preliminaries out of the way, we can now turn to the Internet itself, the major features it offers, and how to use them. It's important to realize up front that the Internet has a *lot* of features. Indeed, the Internet tends to accumulate features the way a rolling snowball picks up rocks, twigs, and other debris.

Some features are wonderful, to be sure, but some are a complete waste of time. The Internet doesn't care. Since there is no central authority that controls the Net, all features are welcome. If you're a computer whiz with an idea for a feature, you can write a program to implement it. If the Net community finds it of value, it will adopt it, and your idea will become a standard feature on the Internet.

Needless to say, however, not every Internet feature is of equal importance in a job search. That's why this chapter has been designed to do double duty. It will acquaint you with the major features of the Internet as a whole, but it will zero in on just those features that are relevant to finding a job on the Internet.

The Prime Concept!

In short, this chapter will prepare you for using the job-finding features detailed in other parts of this book. Starting with what you can think of as the Prime Concept, which is simply this: Virtually everything on the Internet boils down to *addresses*.

If you want to send e-mail to someone, you must know the person's address on the Net. If you want to Telnet to a site, you must know its address. Ditto if you want to FTP to a site or use a specific Gopher or conduct an Archie search. Don't worry about what these terms mean right now. Just keep the concept of "address" firmly in mind.

As we have said before, the geographical location of an Internet *site* or *server* on the face of the globe does not matter. For all practical purposes, all the computers on the Net could be physically located in the room next door. But, like the numbers of the Dewey Decimal System used to keep track of books in a library, *addresses* on the Internet are crucial.

Naturally, there is a method to the apparent madness of the addressing schemes that are used. The Internet is built of computers, after all, and those machines are nothing if not logical and precise. If space permitted, we would be happy to explain this topic in detail. But there's really no point.

Nor is there any point in you spending even a moment's thought on the subject. You will be far better off if you think of an Internet address as an incantation of great power that must be keyed in precisely as given if the magic is to work. That's very much the "cookbook" approach we will take here: Key in *this* address and watch for *that* feature to appear. But first, a tiny touch of history.

 # Internet origins

Physically, the Internet consists of high-speed digital links and the networking software running on the computers that are connected by them. The Net was developed as a U.S. Defense Department project in the 1960s, and its purpose was to link the Pentagon, military bases, defense contractors, and universities in a network that could not be destroyed by a single—or even multiple—atomic blasts.

The effectiveness of this approach was demonstrated during the Gulf War. The Iraqi command and control system was built on the same hardware and software technology that forms the basis of the Internet. And, while no nuclear weapons were used, Allied Forces had a devil of a time knocking it out. Indeed, the Allies never did succeed in shutting it down completely.

Back in this country, as time went on, more and more institutions and businesses hooked themselves up to the Internet. And, with the end of the Cold War and the opening of the Net to the general public, the number of hookups has skyrocketed. Analogies abound, but basically the Internet is like the U.S. interstate highway system—except that no one controls or owns it. The Internet simply *is*.

The Internet today connects millions of individual computers and tens of thousands of computer networks all over the world. But the speed

of communications is so high that in a single online session, you might connect to systems in Switzerland, India, Japan, and the U.S. and not notice any delays or differences. As noted earlier, geographical locations do not matter. In a sense, all points on the Net are the same. Or, to get really metaphysical, there is no "there" on the Net, there is only "here."

The main Internet features

One of the biggest conceptual mistakes any new Net user can make is to assume that the Internet is somehow like a much bigger version of CompuServe, America Online, or one of the other commercial systems. It is not. Instead, it is wild and woolly, delightful and disorganized, eclectic and anarchistic, and anything else you can imagine.

A quick overview

This is great for your co-authors, because it means there is an endless market for books like ours. Yet through it all, a reasonably coherent set of features has developed. Here is a quick overview:

> **Archie**. A program used to search for files by name or partial name. With luck, it will tell you where you can find files with names that meet your criteria on the Net. Once you find a file's location, you can use the FTP feature (see below) to go get it. Searching for a file on the basis of its *name* is the absolute worst way to locate it, yet Archie does indeed work.

> **E-mail**. Use electronic mail to send a message anywhere on the planet in seconds. All commercial online systems can send and receive Internet e-mail these days. So you can reach just about anyone who has a mailbox on just about any system in the world.

> **Newsgroups**. There are some 10,000 newsgroups, each of which is devoted to a specific topic or subtopic. And the topics include everything you can imagine—and, frankly, some topics that you cannot imagine. Questions, answers, information—and

contacts at corporations and other potential employers—are what newsgroups offer job seekers.

➤ **Mailing lists**. Like newsgroups in breadth of topic, but everyone on the list gets every contribution. Another good way to get to know the leading people in your field, or your field of interest.

➤ **FTP**. Used to transfer files to your location, once you find them. The features are not related, but FTP (File Transfer Protocol) is the natural mate for the Archie file-finder feature. It is much more likely, however, that someone will tell you the address of the FTP site to contact and the directory and filename information you need to locate and get a particular file.

➤ **Telnet**. The basic method of logging on to a computer connected to the Internet. What you see once you get there depends on the Telnet address you have used and the program that has been set to run when you enter at that location. A good example is Telnetting to a location and being able to search a college library's card catalogue.

➤ **Gopher**. Probably the most crucial—and most useful—feature on the Net. A Gopher is a menu system that someone has created to make it easier for you to locate and use Internet resources. The two things to remember are that each Gopher menu at each Gopher site is *unique*, and that Gopher menus typically embrace all the other features of the Internet. You can use a Gopher to Telnet to a location or to FTP a file or to do just about anything else—as long as it's on the Gopher menu.

➤ **Veronica** and **Jughead**. Veronica and Jughead are features designed to search the selections on Gopher menus for the keyword you specify. They then present you with a customized Gopher menu, every selection of which contains your keyword. This makes it possible to generate a menu of nothing but job-related Internet resources. The difference between these two features is that Veronica searches a large collection of individual Gopher menus—possibly even all the Gopher menus in existence—and Jughead searches just the Gopher menu at the site you are currently visiting.

➤ **WAIS**. Short for Wide Area Information Server and pronounced "wayz"), WAIS lets you search the *contents* of one or more files for specific words or phrases. This is great. It's just like the kind of powerful searching made available by Lexis/Nexis or Dialog or some other expensive online system of databases. Unfortunately, WAIS is offered only by certain servers, and it can thus be applied to only a limited number of information files.

WAIS databases also include *hypertext links* that let you click on a highlighted word or phrase and be taken to some thematically linked collection of data. In theory, this is wonderful. In practice, there is the problem that any and all hypertext links must be inserted by human beings. So, if your own way of thinking is in synch with the person who prepared the hypertext file, great. If not, then, not so great. In the latter case, you may look at a person's name or at a phrase and wonder why on earth there is no "hot button" hypertext link attached to it!

➤ **World Wide Web (WWW)**. As noted in Chapter 1, the World Wide Web is designed to turn your computer screen into a magazine page, complete with fancy text fonts, photos, and graphics. You will also find hypertext hot buttons that link you to other pages, features, or information. All you have to do is click.

Unfortunately, despite the hype in the largely uninformed, lazy, laymen's press, the World Wide Web is simply unusable for most people. If you're one of the rare breed who has access to a high-speed T1 or T3 connection to the Internet, the Web is absolutely divine. If not—if you are stuck using the 14.4 and 28.8 connections available to the common person at this time—you can go gray waiting for a single Web page to paint itself on your screen!

Thus, the best way to use the Web is to make turning off the graphics your first task whenever you connect to a Web site. (If the specific Web site does not permit this, check to see if you

can turn off graphics using your own Web browser software.)
To which you might say, "Well, then, if you turn off the
graphics, what's the point of the Web?" And to which we
would respond, "Exactly! What *is* the point of the World Wide
Web?"

➡ The main job-related features

There simply is not space to go into detail. Therefore, you must take
it on faith that each of the features cited here (and those few minor
features not mentioned) have become available on the Internet over
time almost by accident. No market studies were done. No focus
group discussions were held. No controlling intelligence was involved
at all. The features more or less just "happened."

Archie is a good example. As the authors of numerous books and
articles about "how to look it up online," we can say with conviction
that searching for something on the basis of its *filename* is about as
crude and inaccurate an approach as one can imagine. Yet in a crazy
kind of way, it does work on the Net, particularly if someone has
already told you exactly what filename to search for. So the Archie
concept has been adopted and turned into a "feature" by the Internet
community.

But for you to use the Internet as a job-finding resource, there is
really no need for you to learn the many features and variations
Archie provides. The same logic applies to FTP, Telnet, Veronica and
Jughead, WAIS, and the World Wide Web.

Trust us. As we encounter these features in the chapters ahead, we
will tell you exactly what to do. But there is simply no need for any
normal person to master all the ins and outs—all the switches and
fancy commands—these features offer. For a job seeker, learning all
of these intricate details is just a waste of time.

Areas of concentration

For a job-seeker, only certain Internet features are really worth learning to use:

- E-mail
- Newsgroups
- Mailing lists
- Telnet
- Gopher
- The World Wide Web

You need to know how to use e-mail effectively so you can communicate with prospective employers and industry contacts. You need to know how to use newsgroups and mailing lists so you can identify key players and make contacts in your industry or field of interest. And you need a firm grounding in the menu-driven Gopher approach to the Internet because it is likely to be the most crucial feature of all.

As for the Web, you need to know about it because, well, because it's there and everyone's talking about it. And you will certainly want to give it a try. But, in most cases, you will find that there is nothing on any Web site that you cannot obtain faster and with less fuss some other way.

In any case, these six features are likely to prove most essential to your online job quest. And each is explained in the next chapter. The goal of Chapter 4 is to give you a good basic grounding in these features, the better to equip you for the real-life online versions we'll explore in Part 2.

How to use the tools

IF you have read this far, you are at least marginally aware that the Internet is quite rich in features, but that not all available features are equally good or equally applicable to a job search.

Having surveyed the field with job searching in mind, then, the features of greatest importance are:

➢ E-mail

➢ Newsgroups

➢ Mailing lists

➢ Telnet

➢ Gopher

➢ The World Wide Web

All of this you know from Chapter 3. Here we will cover them one by one, giving you the essential information you need to understand and use them. Then, in Chapter 5, we will show you how some of these features can be used to tap the Net in a subject-specific way.

 # Basic e-mail, all systems

The electronic mail concept could not be simpler. You call into a given online system and key in or upload a message. That online system prompts you for an e-mail address and subject line. And, after you satisfy those requests, your message is sent on its way to your addressee.

If your correspondent has an account on the same system, say, CompuServe, then the message you upload really doesn't go anywhere. It sits in a storage area with a flag attached to it indicating that "This message is for John Smith." When John Smith signs onto CompuServe the next time, he will be notified that he has electronic mail waiting. He can choose to ignore this, but more than likely he will key in go mail to enter the mail system on CompuServe and read your message.

But suppose John Smith is on Delphi instead of CompuServe. Or suppose he's on America Online (AOL). Or some other system.

Well, here's where the advent of universal Internet access genuinely improves the quality of all of our lives. To wit: Prior to the Internet being opened to the public, if you wanted to correspond with John Smith on CompuServe, both you and he had to have accounts on that system. (It's true that one of you could have been on MCI Mail, but let's not muddy the waters right now.)

Today, with the Internet serving as the common carrier, you can be on Prodigy and send an e-mail message via the Internet to John Smith on AOL, and he can forward it, via the Internet, to someone on any other system. In short, thanks to the Internet, all online systems are essentially linked for electronic mail.

This is a remarkable accomplishment in the eyes of those of us who have watched the online world for some years. All is still not as easy as one might hope. There are some wrinkles. But if you've used e-mail of any sort, you already know what to do:

❶ Prepare your message with your favorite word processor, but make sure that you save it as *plain ASCII text*. (Your software may use the term "non-document mode" or "unformatted text.)

❷ Sign on to your chosen online service and get into its mail program.

❸ Tell the program you want to send mail, and respond to the resulting prompt with the e-mail address of your recipient.

❹ Transmit your previously prepared text file, and then enter the required command to tell the system that you have completed your message.

❺ The system may ask if you are satisfied with your message. If you say you are, the message will be sent.

❻ Finally, to read mail someone has sent to you, sign on to the system, get to the mail feature, open your comm program's *capture buffer* so the text you are about to receive will be recorded on your hard drive, and then choose the option to read your mail. Usually, you will be able to key in a reply on the spot, if you feel so moved.

 # Points to watch

The specific details differ, but all e-mail works in essentially this way. There are also some key points to remember about all e-mail systems. First and most important: plain, 7-bit, ASCII text is the *lingua franca* of electronic mail. That essentially means that only the characters you can type from your keyboard can be used.

Many beginners make the mistake of thinking that the perfectly formatted messages they create in WordPerfect, Word, or some other program are what will be displayed on their correspondents' screens. Unfortunately, if you fail to save your message in plain ASCII text, your correspondent will see your text interspersed with "garbage" characters on the screen.

If you *must* send someone a WordPerfect or similar document with all its special codes and formatting intact, you must send it as a *binary file*, and you cannot use Internet e-mail to do so. At least you cannot do so without first converting it to 7-bit ASCII text using a program like UUENCODE (available from Glossbrenner's Choice on the "Internet 6" disk, and from many other sources).

Second, you can get PC or Mac software that will automate much of the process just outlined. That software will include a text editor or word processor for preparing your messages offline, and it will be smart enough to prompt you for the subject line and e-mail address you want to use.

This makes it possible for you to prepare a batch of letters and then tell the software to sign on and automatically mail them. If the program finds that you have mail in your mailbox, it will automatically pick it up and notify you of the fact. Then it will sign off.

Needless to say, this is the most efficient way to handle e-mail.

Since you compose offline, with no connect-time meter ticking, no cost is involved. Plus you have the time to write a really thoughtful letter, if appropriate. On the other hand, if most of the letters you get require only a quick response, you may be better off telling your

software that you want to read each message in turn and respond to it on the spot.

 # Dot-crazy addresses on the Net

Now let's consider those crazy Internet mail addresses that are starting to appear in company ads and in magazine and newspaper articles. The tip-off that it's an Internet address is the "at" sign (@). Internet addresses consist of two parts: the stuff to the left of the "at" sign and the stuff to its right.

As an example, let's take a look at the Internet address **grendel@beowulf.heorot.com**. If Grendel were giving you his address, he would say, "I'm Grendel at Beowulf dot Heorot dot Com." But Internet computers read this kind of address from right to left. So the address tells them (and us) that the location is a commercial system called Heorot, on a computer called Beowulf that's part of that system. And Grendel is the "logon" name of the individual person.

The information to the right of the "at" sign is called the *domain*. Internet addresses all follow the *Domain Name System* of addressing. Most addresses you'll see end in one of the following *zone* name extensions:

.com   U.S. commercial businesses
.edu   U.S. college and university sites
.gov   Governmental bodies
.int   International bodies, like NATO
.mil   Military organizations
.net   Companies or organizations that run large networks
.org   Nonprofit organizations and others that don't fit anywhere else

Moving to the left, following the zone is the organization's name—in this case, Heorot. If the organization is a large one, it may have several computers or network servers, each with its own name. In this case, the computer at the Heorot organization where Grendel hangs out is called Beowulf.

The Internet mail system effectively "reads" these addresses from right to left. The computers that route and transport the mail know that it is their responsibility to deliver a message to the "highest" subdomain in the full domain name, in this case, the Heorot system. After that, it is the responsibility of the subdomain name system to take over routing and transport within its own network.

 # IP addresses

The Domain Name System is actually a mask that hides the *numerical* addresses the Internet Protocol (IP) actually uses. Somewhere along the way to our friend Grendel, one or more Internet *nameserver* computers will convert the Domain Name System address **grendel@beowulf.heorot.com** into something like **Grendel@123.45.67.89**. This might translate as "network number 123.45, and computer 67.89 on that network."

For computers, it's easy. For humans, it's not. So the Domain Name System was invented to let us use plain English to specify the same thing.

 # How to send mail to other networks

Many subscribers to the major consumer systems, MCI Mail, and most Internet access providers are still not aware of the connectivity that exists today to allow the exchange of e-mail among the various systems. Here's a quick primer on how to send mail among systems using the Internet as a common carrier.

✳ **America Online (AOL)** To send mail to someone on AOL, remove any spaces from the person's AOL user name and add **@aol.com** to get an address like **jsmith@aol.com**. (If you don't know the user name, your best bet is to call the person and ask.)

To send mail from America Online to someone on the Internet, just put the person's Internet address in the "To" field before composing your message.

✳ **CompuServe** CompuServe users have numerical addresses in the form **12345,678**. To send mail to a CompuServe user, change the comma to a period and add **@compuserve.com** to get an address like **12345.678@compuserve.com**. (Keep in mind that most CompuServe users must pay a minimum of fifteen cents for each message received from the Internet.)

To send mail from CompuServe to someone on the Internet, use an address in the form **>INTERNET:jsmith@company.org**. The colon (:) is required.

✳ **Delphi Internet Services** To send mail to a Delphi subscriber, use an address consisting of the person's Delphi user name plus **@delphi.com** to get an address like **jsmith@delphi.com**.

To send mail from Delphi to someone on the Internet, the form is **internet"jsmith@company.org"** (The quotation marks are required).

✳ **GEnie** To send mail to a GEnie user, add **@genie.geis.com** to the end of the GEnie user name, for example: **jsmith@genie.geis.com**.

To send mail from the GEnie Mail system to someone on the Internet, use the person's Internet address plus the constant **INET#**. The address will look like this: **jsmith@company.org@INET#**.

✳ **MCI Mail** To send mail to someone with an MCI Mail account, add **@mcimail.com** to the end of the person's name or numerical address. For example: **555-1234@mcimail.com** or **jsmith@mcimail.com**. (You're better off using the numerical address if the person has a relatively common name, since there can be no doubt about the John Smith at 555-1234, but considerable doubt about JSMITH.)

To send mail from MCI Mail to an Internet address, at the "To:" prompt, key in the person's name and (EMS). At the resulting "EMS:" prompt, key in internet. At the resulting "MBX:" prompt, key in the recipient's Internet address.

✳ **Prodigy** To send mail to a Prodigy user, add **@prodigy.com** to the person's Prodigy user ID. For example: **jsmith@prodigy.com**. (As with CompuServe, Prodigy users must pay extra for Internet e-mail.)

To send mail from Prodigy to an Internet address, you'll need Mail Manager software, which is available for download from Prodigy. After composing your message offline using Mail Manager, send it to the person's normal Internet address, like **jsmith@company.org**. No special punctuation is required.

Making the most of newsgroups

If electronic mail is the most used Internet feature, *newsgroups*—and to a lesser extent mailing lists—are certainly the most popular. Both can provide you with an incredible amount of truly incredible information about a field of interest and some of the leading players in that field.

From a job seeker's perspective, newsgroups offer a wonderful way to learn about a given industry, profession, or issue. And, once you've learned the basics, the rest is easy because all newsgroups operate alike.

Newsgroup essentials

Internet newsgroups are such a major factor on the Net that we could easily write a book about them alone. But here are the bare facts everyone must know:

➢ The "news" in "newsgroups" originally referred to news about the Internet or online networking or other techno-topics. These days, news as news has very little to do with most newsgroups, although the name remains.

➢ Conceptually, newsgroups are merely "player piano rolls" of messages, or *articles* in Netspeak. Each group is devoted to some topic. The comments Internet users may want to make about that topic are posted one after the other into a long player piano roll.

➤ No one controls the newsgroups. The notes people post circulate like bits of dust in the jet stream. The flow of messages among Internet sites is constant, and that stream encompasses the entire world.

➤ The only filtering that takes place is when a given site administrator decides not to accept or make available to users the contents of certain groups. America Online, for example, does not carry the sexually-oriented groups. Prodigy does carry them, but to gain access, you've got to officially acknowledge that you are aware that they contain adult material.

➤ Millions of people read the *netnews* (newsgroup postings) daily. But no one reads *every* group. The software used to read netnews keeps track of the groups you have chosen to read regularly and which messages in those groups you have not yet read. That way you don't have to start from the beginning every time you sign on.

➤ Anyone can post a new article or a reply to an article on almost any group. Taken together, a new article and the replies (and replies to replies) it generates form a *message thread*.

The only limitations are that the postings be appropriate to the group, that no single posting be longer than the equivalent of about 15 single-spaced pages of text, and that you use plain, 7-bit ASCII text.

How to get a comprehensive list

One thing you will quickly learn about the Net is that there is a FAQ (Frequently Asked Questions) file or a list for nearly everything. In the case of newsgroups, the FAQ is called Answers to Frequently Asked Questions about Usenet, and it is posted regularly to the newsgroups **news.announce.newusers** and **news.answers**.

The original list of newsgroups was created by Gene Spafford and then taken on by David C. Lawrence. The list comes in several parts: two parts for the alternative (ALT) groups and two for everything else. As a convenience, all of these files are available on the

Newsgroup Essentials disk (Internet 4) from Glossbrenner's Choice. Or, you can get them via FTP or newsgroup postings:

➢ FTP to **ftp.uu.net**

- Path: /usenet/news.answers/alt-hierarchies/

- Path: /usenet/news.answers/active-newsgroups/

➢ Check these newsgroups:

- news.lists

- news.groups

- news.announce.newgroups

- news.answers

➡ Searching offline

Once you've got the comprehensive list of newsgroups on your disk, the next step is to identify the ones most likely to be of interest. That way, you will be able to tell your newsreader program exactly which group to go to.

So, with your list of newsgroups on disk, it just makes sense to use your computer's power to search it. The program we like for this purpose is Vernon Buerg's famous shareware LIST program, but any word processing program with a "search" function will do. Just key in any topic that occurs to you, and activate the search function.

Major newsgroup hierarchies

To make it easier for people to find what they're looking for, Usenet newsgroups are divided into topics. Each main topic is further divided, and the result is often divided again and again, as areas are created for discussions of ever greater specificity.

*For example, a group called **alt.music** might be formed to discuss music in general. But as people really get into the swing of things, some may decide that they really want to focus on baroque or jazz or hip-hop. So **alt.music.baroque** might be formed, along with **alt.music.jazz** and **alt.music.hip-hop**. And so on.*

Here are the main topic categories of Usenet newsgroups likely to be of greatest interest to job seekers:

alt   *Alternative newsgroups. Basically, topics that don't fit neatly anywhere else. Many Usenet sites don't carry these groups.*

biz   *The accepted place for advertisements, marketing, and other commercial postings. Product announcements, product reviews, demo software, and so forth.*

comp *Topics of interest to both computer professionals and hobbyists, including computer science, software source code, and information on hardware and software systems.*

misc *Groups addressing themes not easily classified under any of the other headings or which incorporate themes from multiple categories.*

rec   *Groups oriented towards the arts, hobbies, and recreational activities.*

sci   *Discussions relating to research in or application of the established sciences.*

soc   *Groups primarily addressing social issues and socializing.*

Mailing lists

Now let's consider Internet *mailing lists*. These work just like a conventional mailing list—once your name has been added to a list, messages relevant to the list will begin to appear in your electronic mailbox automatically.

Mailing lists can be a wonderful source of information on a given subject. If you are interested in some technical or theoretical aspect of an industry, for example, you may discover that joining the right mailing list is like becoming a member of a perpetual symposium.

Getting a list of lists

The key thing is to find out which mailing lists exist and which pertain to the topic or industry or profession of greatest interest. In

the long tradition of the Internet, what you need is a list of lists—mailing lists, that is.

Two of the most comprehensive lists of mailing lists are the SRI List of Lists by Vivian Neou, and PAML (Publicly Accessible Mailing Lists) by Stephanie Da Silva. To get the SRI List, send an e-mail message to **mail-server@sri.com**. Include the line "send interest-groups" in the body of the message. For PAML, check the newsgroups **news.lists** or **news.answers**, where it is posted periodically.

As a convenience, both of these lists are also available from Glossbrenner's Choice on a disk called Mailing List Essentials (Internet 5). This disk also includes DOS search software to make it easy to find mailing lists of interest. Each listing typically includes the instructions you must follow to subscribe. Usually it is a simple matter of sending a special e-mail message to a given address.

 # Telnet, the simplest command of all

Telnet is simply the name for the procedure by which you connect to a given computer site on the Net. You tell your software or access location to run Telnet and respond to the resulting prompt with your target address. That's all there is to it.

What you see next depends entirely on the program running at the site you have specified. It might be a program to let you search a college library's card catalog. Or it might be a Gopher menu system. (Telnet is what gets you to a Gopher site; Gopher is the software you encounter once you get there.)

For example, if you want an instant weather report, activate Telnet and specify the following as the target address: **downwind.sprl.umich.edu 3000**. The "3000" at the end of the address is the *port number* you've got to specify to tell the remote system which program to run.

Most Telnet and Gopher sites do indeed have port numbers, but much of the time you do not have to include it in the address. Unless, of course, you are specifically told to do so. Should you be taken by surprise by a request for a port number when using Gopher, try specifying port 70. By convention, this is the port many Gopher host programs are designed to use.

Telnetting to various locations is a lot of fun. And it's easy. The only twist is that some locations expect to be "talking to" a DEC VT-100 terminal. That shouldn't be a problem if you Telnet directly from a computer center terminal. But if you are connecting via modem with your own computer, check your communications software to see what you must do to *emulate* a VT-100. If you can, make this emulation your permanent setting, since it normally will not interfere with most other, non-VT-100 online sessions.

 # Using Gopher

In our opinion, the single most outstanding feature on the Internet is the Gopher menu system. As we'll see here and in later chapters, Gophers give you fast and easy access to almost *every* other feature on the Net. Once you've tried a Gopher, we think you'll agree that it is the most important Internet feature of all.

The Gopher concept was dreamed up by some real computer geniuses at the University of Minnesota. Gopher software is available free of charge to any Internet site requesting it, but it arrives as an empty shell. The system administrators at each Gopher site are the ones responsible for creating that location's Gopher menu.

That site-specific menu can embrace all aspects of the Net—from Telnet to FTP to other Gophers and more. And, of course, there are menus and submenus, and sub-submenus. The key points to remember are these:

❶ Each Gopher menu is unique. So, naturally, the Gophers at some sites are more complete and comprehensive than those at others. If your Internet access provider does not have a specific Gopher feature, look for a Telnet feature. You can access all Gopher sites

by means of Telnet. All you need is the proper address. (See the nearby sidebar on Gopher servers.)

❷ Gopher menu items don't just tell you about some item or feature—they go get it! Which is to say, they "go fer" it. Thus, if you select an item like "Jobs for Programmers in Hawaii," you will be connected to the Internet location that has those files. Indeed, you might pick that item and then be shown a list of companies with positions available.

Choose one, and the Gopher might actually connect to the remote site and get the file containing the job description for you. This would eliminate the need to horse around with the Internet's FTP feature—your friendly Gopher would take care of everything.

❸ You can access most Gopher sites in at least two ways. You can opt for "All the Gophers in the World," a selection you will find on most Gopher menus. You can then click on a particular Gopher site, or key in a Gopher address (like **occ.com**) to get to the Online Career Center Gopher. This will produce a plain text menu.

Alternatively, you can use a World Wide Web browser like Netscape Navigator or Netcom's NetCruiser. The trick is to click on File and then on Open Location (or your browser program's equivalent). Then specify the target Gopher location as a URL (Uniform Resource Locator).

For example, if you want to reach the Online Career Center Gopher using your Web browser program, you would specify **gopher://occ.com**. The word "gopher," the colon, and the two forward slashes are crucial to the URL specification.

Gophers everywhere!

Gopher software is so popular that Gopher servers have sprung up everywhere. At this writing, America Online, Delphi, and all independent Internet service providers give you access to Gopherspace. That means you can activate the Gopher feature and select some popular Gopher site from a menu, or opt to access "All the Gophers in the World" and key in the address of your own preferred Gopher location.

*If this is not the case, however, there are publicly available Gopher sites. You will find the most recent list in the Gopher FAQ (Frequently Asked Questions) file available by FTP from numerous places on the Internet. Or you might check the newsgroups **news.answers** or **comp.answers**.*

Here are some of the publicly available Gopher sites accessible via Telnet. Specify one of these addresses as your desired Telnet location and respond with that site's "login" when you are prompted for it. Use the site nearest you to minimize network lag and traffic.

Site Address	Login	Area
consultant.micro.umn.edu	gopher	North America
ux1.cso.uiuc.edu	gopher	North America
panda.uiowa.edu	panda	North America
gopher.msu.edu	gopher	North America
tolten.puc.cl	gopher	South America
ecnet.ec	gopher	Ecuador
gopher.ebone.net	gopher	Europe
gopher.sunet.se	gopher	Sweden
info.anu.edu.au	info	Australia
gan.ncc.go.jp	gopher	Japan

Working with your friendly Gopher

Gopher—plus Veronica and Jughead, the two tools that search Gopher menu items—are the main "finding" features on the Internet. There is not a great deal to say about how to use them. After all, they are designed to be intuitive.

The screens you see when you access a Gopher usually depend on your means of access and on the version of the Gopher program a given site is using. If you use your World Wide Web browser to log onto a Gopher site, as mentioned earlier, you will be able to use your mouse to move up and down the lists of menu items and select items by clicking on them.

If you Telnet to a Gopher site, you may see a pointer (-->) that you can move up and down the left margin of the menu. Usually, though, there is no reason to do so, since you can select any item by keying in its number and hitting your Enter key.

The pointer can be important for the more advanced Gopher commands, however. It signifies the *current item*. As you will see when you enter the question mark to get a Gopher command summary, there are lots of ways to move the pointer and go from one menu page to the next. Here are just the basics using lowercase letters:

➤ To move the pointer down one item, hit j.

➤ To move it up one item, hit k.

➤ To move to the next page of a menu, hit your Spacebar.

➤ To move back a page (to back up) hit u.

 # Information and Bookmark commands

You may or may not wish to invest the time needed to completely master all Gopher commands. But two commands not to be missed are the *Information command* and the *Bookmark command*.

With the pointer at, say, "12. CIA World Factbook," you can hit your equals key (=) and Gopher will reveal the Internet commands that are "attached" to that entry. (On the Delphi Gopher, the command to use to learn about item 12 is info 12.)

In this case, you'd learn that the host the Gopher Telnets to is **info.umd.edu**, entry port **901**. And that the path it then follows is 1/info/Government/Factbook. This is the information you need to go do this yourself, should a Gopher be unavailable.

The Bookmark command lets you create your own customized Gopher menu. (You may see these identified as your "Personal Favorites" on some systems.) Simply move the pointer to an item and hit a to add the item to your list. Hitting a capital A adds the current

menu to your list. (On the Delphi Gopher, the command to use is save.)

To start Gopher using your personal Bookmark list, key in gopher -b at your system's prompt. To jump to your Bookmark list after you've started Gopher by just keying in gopher, key in v for "view bookmark list."

If you're using a World Wide Web browser like Mosaic or Netscape Navigator, look for the Information and Bookmark commands on the pull-down menus.

 # The Web: Good & bad, but always good-looking

Now let's turn to the World Wide Web. The industry and media hype has made the Web unavoidable. And you can see why. The screens (once they arrive on your system) are usually very attractive—the way Windows and the Macintosh are attractive when compared to the plain text of DOS.

Also, the concept of *hypertext links* is enthralling. Imagine starting from a *home page* (or opening screen) devoted to food. You click on an icon for Cajun and are taken to a site in New Orleans, where a new page appears offering you recipes for various Cajun dishes.

That New Orleans Web page might include an option to explore classic French cuisine. Click on that, and you are taken to a location in Paris with a Web page offering tips from the great chefs, recipes, and possibly a glossary of French cooking terms.

You could go on like this for hours, hopscotching around the globe from one World Wide Web home page to another, clicking on whatever item interested you and letting your curiosity be your guide.

Sounds wonderful. Who wouldn't be enthusiastic about the World Wide Web? Someone who has actually tried it, that's who. The Web as described here is a dream that is a long, long way from realization.

In fact, we have no hesitation in saying that the Web as it exists today simply is "not ready for prime time."

 # Two Web problems

You will definitely want to try accessing the Web, and we have included many screen shots and instructions to make it easy for you to do so. Just don't expect a miracle. Don't believe the hype.

At least two problems exist. One is the generally inept design of many Web sites. The HTML (Hypertext Markup Language) used to create World Wide Web home pages is not difficult to learn, so almost anyone can create an impressive looking Web page. Just as anyone can make the worst piece of writing look good by bringing the text into a desktop publishing program.

But in both cases, the good looks are often superficial. The problem with creating a really good Web page is the same faced when writing any computer program: anticipating user needs and actions and thinking long and hard about how people will actually work with and use the product.

Those are precisely the steps so many of today's Web home page programmers have neglected to take. Consequently, you will find many a Web page that is so full of large graphic images or photos that five or ten minutes are required to send it to you over the phone lines. When you encounter such a page, you cannot help wondering, "Didn't anybody at the site try this thing themselves?" The answer has got to be, "Er, uh, no."

As similar evidence of the amateurish nature of most Web pages, most do not give you the option of speeding things up by turning off the graphics. You have to know enough to be able to do this yourself with your own local Web browser software.

The second big problem is that graphic images of any size take some time to transmit, even if you are connected using a 28.8 kbps SLIP/PPP connection. That's the highest speed available for data communications over normal phone lines, and even then the Web is just barely usable. Unless you can knit, watch TV, or read the paper while you wait for screens to be painted, accessing the World Wide Web is not a way most people would willingly spend their time.

 # URLs: Uniform Resource Locators

You may or may not choose to use the Web on a regular basis. But you still need to know that URL is short for Uniform Resource Locator, and it will come up in nearly any discussion of the World Wide Web and the Internet in general. This is a draft standard for specifying an "object" on the Internet. The object can be anything—a file, a Gopher site, a newsgroup, a Web site, and so forth.

URLs are thus informative addresses that, in a single expression, tell you the kind of object and where it can be found. Here's an example:

```
file://wuarchive.wustl.edu/mirrors/msdos/graphics/gifkit.zip
```

This URL tells you that the file "gifkit.zip" can be found at the **wuarchive.wustl.edu** site, along the specified path. The two slashes after the colon indicate that a machine name follows, in this case "wuarchive.wustl.edu." The URL address **http://info.cern.ch:80/default.html** specifies a World Wide Web site and HTML hypertext file. The "http" stands for Hypertext Transport Protocol. That's the tipoff that it's a Web site. And, as mentioned earlier, *html* stands for *Hypertext Markup Language*, the page-description language used to prepare Web-accessible documents.

 # Tips for using a Web browser

Figure 4-1 offers a good example of one of the more elaborate World Wide Web pages you are likely to find. This is the Web home page for CareerMosaic, a feature sponsored by Bernard Hodes Advertising, Inc. We'll tell you all about CareerMosaic in Chapter 12. For now, notice the URL in the "Location" box at the top of the screen. This tells you that if you want to go to this site, you must tell Netscape or whatever Web browser program you are using to take you to the URL **http://www.careermosaic.com/**.

Figure 4-1

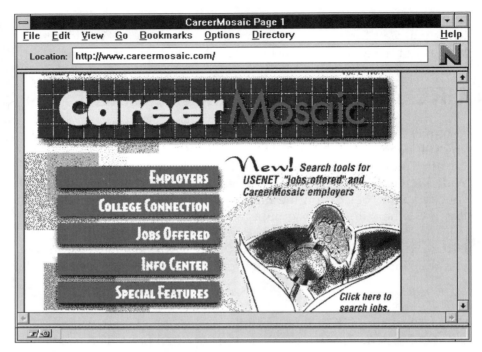

CareerMosaic's flashy home page.

Check your Web browsing software to see if you can click on File and then select Open URL or Open Location. Key in the URL *exactly* as you see it in print. Keep in mind that URL expressions are *case-sensitive.* That means that if you were to specify the address as **http://WWW.CareerMosaic.com**/, it will not work.

You will want to play with your Web browser package, of course. But at some point early on, take the time to figure out how to save a Web page as a file. This will probably be as simple as clicking on File and then on "Save as…" or "Save." Your browser will save the file and give it the extension .HTM, as in CAREER.HTM or some other name.

There are two important things you can do with .HTM files. First, you can use your browser program to view them later. Click on File and then on Open and specify the file's name. The file will be displayed, graphics and all, just as if you were online and logged onto that site.

Second, .HTM files contain all the HTML instructions needed to tell a Web browser what and how to display them. That means they contain a lot of HTML text that gets in the way when you want to treat an .HTM file as a text file. The solution to this is the DE-HTML.EXE program that you will find on the Glossbrenner's Choice disk Internet 8, World Wide Web Essentials. This program will quickly strip out all HTML codes and commands. Bring the resulting file into your word processor and adjust the paragraphs to your desired margins, and you'll be all set.

The Internet

Organized by subject

CHAPTER 5

NOW that you have an acquaintance with the most important tools the Internet offers to aid you in your job search, let's see how they can be used to get real information out of the Net. This may be general information about a company or an industry, or it may be job- and employment-related information. In this chapter we make no distinctions. The key thing is to be aware of and get comfortable with these information-finding resources.

When it comes to subject-specific information on the Internet, the good news and the bad news are the same: There is more of it on every conceivable subject than you will ever be able to find.

Fortunately, longtime Internet users are well aware of this. That's why some of them have taken it upon themselves to produce lists and guides. It's also why, no matter where you land, you'll find many people who will voluntarily point you to other related resources. One thing, in other words, almost always leads to another.

As you will quickly discover, you don't have to find *everything* on the Net related to your field of interest. All you have to do is find what you need. And to do that, you must have a starting point. That's what you'll find in this chapter—a starting point. Lots of starting points in fact. (In later chapters you will find even more specific, job-related information.)

In this chapter, we will introduce you to four truly excellent resources:

> ➤ The Rice University Gopher (RiceInfo)
> ➤ The Clearinghouse for Subject-Oriented Internet Resource Guides
> ➤ The Gopher Jewels
> ➤ The Library of Congress MARVEL Gopher

The resources available through the Internet are so vast that any number of attempts have been made to get a handle on things. After all, information doesn't do anybody any good if no one can find it or even knows it's there. The best printed reference we have seen is *The Internet Yellow Pages* by Harley Hahn and Rick Stout (Osborne/McGraw-Hill). But for online access, the features profiled here are hard to beat.

 # The RiceInfo Gopher

The folks at Houston's William Marsh Rice University have built a Gopher that is specifically designed to present Internet resources by *subject area*. They call it, naturally enough, the RiceInfo Gopher. To get to it, Gopher to **riceinfo.rice.edu** and choose "Information by Subject Area" from the menu. (The Web version can be found at the URL **http://riceinfo.rice.edu/**.)

Selecting "Information by Subject Area" (Item 9 when we were there) on the main RiceInfo Gopher menu leads to over 40 subject-specific submenus. The first six selections from the first menu page are shown here, but to save space, we have stripped out everything but the actual subject items for the succeeding entries. Just keep in mind that each subject item on the list will lead you to a submenu containing items and resources related to that subject. (Notice that one of the subjects is "Jobs & Employment;" we'll have more to say about that in Chapter 11.)

```
                  Information by Subject Area (RiceInfo)
1. About the RiceInfo collection of "Info. by Subject Area"    Text
2. More about "Information by Subject Area"                    Menu
3. Clearinghouse of Subject-Oriented Internet Resource Guides  Meun
4. Search all of Gopherspace by title: Jughead (from WLU)      Search
5. Search all of Gopherspace by title: Veronica               Menu
6. Search all of RiceInfo by title: Jughead                   Menu
```

Aerospace
Agriculture & Forestry
Anthropology & Culture
Architecture
Arts
Astronomy & Astrophysics

Biology
Census
Chemistry
Computer Networks/Internet Guides
Computing
Economics & Business
Education
Engineering
Environment & Ecology

Grants, Scholarships, & Funding
History
Jobs & Employment
Language & Linguistics
Library & Information Science
Literature, Electronic Books, &
   Journals
Mathematics
Medicine & Health
Military Science
Music
News & Journalism
Oceanography
Physics
Reference
Religion & Philosophy

Film & Television	Scholarly Societies (from U Waterloo)
Geography	Sociology & Psychology
Geology & Geophysics	Travel
Government, Political Science, & Law	Weather, Climate, & Meteorology

 # The Clearinghouse for Subject-Oriented Internet Resource Guides

The University of Michigan's University Library and the School of Information and Library Studies (SILS) have established a system for creating and distributing some truly incredible subject-oriented guides to Internet resources. The full title of this project is given in the headline above. Here we'll just call it the "Clearinghouse."

At this writing over 160 guides are available. More are sure to have been added by the time you read this. The guides are prepared by longtime Internauts and by SILS students working under a faculty advisor as part of the Internet Resource Discovery Project.

Although they vary in quality and comprehensiveness, most are on the order of 20 pages or more of single-spaced text. And they typically cover *everything*: Gophers, Telnet sites, World Wide Web home pages, files you can FTP, newsgroups, mailing lists, bulletin board systems—the works!

 ## How to get to the Clearinghouse

There are lots of ways to get to the Clearinghouse at the University of Michigan. Perhaps the easiest is to simply pick the relevant item off your local Gopher. If your Gopher doesn't have such, use the RiceInfo Gopher (**riceinfo.rice.edu**). As you can see on the "Information by Subject Area (RiceInfo)" list presented earlier in this chapter, Item 3 will take you to the Clearinghouse. You can also get there by FTP, Gopher, Telnet, and the World Wide Web:

➤ FTP to **una.hh.lib.umich.edu**; Path: /inetdirsstacks/. Then get the file called .README-FOR-FTP. Or simply use the DIR command. The filenames in this directory are self-explanatory.

➤ Gopher to **gopher.lib.umich.edu** and select "What's New and Featured Resources" and then "Clearinghouse . . ."

➤ Telnet to **una.hh.lib.umich.edu 70**.

➤ Use World Wide Web browser software to visit one of these two URLs. Note the tilde (~) before the letters *lou* in the second address:

http://www.lib.umich.edu/chhome.html

http://http2.sils.umich.edu/~lou/chhome.html

Figure 5-1 will give you an idea of what you can expect when you tap into the Clearinghouse via the Web.

 ## Clearinghouse topics

In our opinion, the fastest, most satisfying way to access the Clearinghouse is via Gopher. When you access it this way, you will get a short opening menu that contains a selection for "Clearinghouse for Subject-Oriented Internet Resource Guides." Choose it, and you will see a submenu that looks like this:

```
Clearinghouse for Subject-Oriented Internet Resource Guides
(UMich) Page 1 of 1

1    About the Clearinghouse (UMich)                      Menu
2    Search full texts of these Guides                    Search
3    All Guides                                           Menu
4      Guides on the Humanities                           Menu
5      Guides on the Sciences                             Menu
6      Guides on the Social Sciences                      Menu
7    The Internet Resource Discovery Project (UMich)      Menu
8    Helpful Information on using the Internet            Menu
9    Clearinghouse Updates (last updated 01/11/95)  (UMich)  Text

Enter Item Number, SAVE, ?, or BACK: 3
```

Figure 5-1

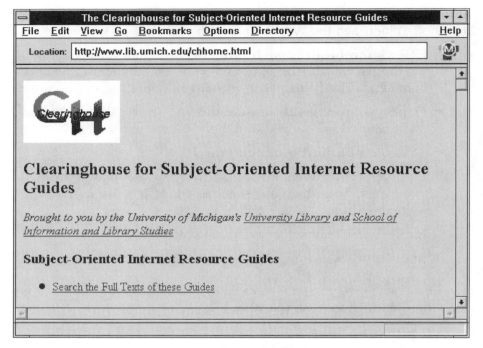

The Clearinghouse home page on the World Wide Web.

Choose Item 3 from this menu to display a list of all the subject-specific guides. Here's a sampling:

```
All Guides
Page 1 of 1

1   Search full texts of these guides                           Search
2   Academic Computing Training & User Support; M. Kovacs; v8; 0   Text
3   Adult/Distance Education; J. Ellsworth; 07/01/94            Text
4   Aerospace Engineering; C. Poterala, D. Dalquist; v2; 3/15/94   Text
5   Agriculture, Veterinary Science & Zoology; L. Haas; v8; 03/9   Text
6   Agriculture; W. Drew; v4.0; 08/08/94                        Text
7   Alternative Medicine; J. Makulowich; 07/29/94               Text
8   Anesthesia & Critical Care; A. Wright; v17; 12/26/94        Text
9   Animals; K. Boschert; v3.0; 06/01/94                        Text
10  Anthropology, Cross Cultural Studies, & Archaeology; G. Bell   Text
11  Aquatic Biology; B. Brown; v2; 07/04/94                     Text
12  Archaeology, Historic Preservation; P. Stott; v3.08; 01/07/9   Text
13  Architecture, Building; J. Brown; 01/95                     Text
14  Archives; D. Anthony, N. Kayne; v2; 05/27/94   (UMich)      Text
15  Art & Architecture; K. Robinson; v8; 03/94                  Text...
(etc.)
```

The "All Guides" menu goes on to include a total of over 160 selections. Everything from Black/African to Buddhism, Conservation, Film and Video, Journalism, Law, Medical Resources, Midwifery, Tibetan Studies, and West European History and Culture.

Remember, each of these guides consists of *lists* and *descriptions* of Internet subject-specific resources. You won't find information on, say, botany, here. But you *will* find a file that tells you where to look on the Net for information about botany and botanical subjects. Also, notice that the very first selection on the All Guides menu is "Search full texts of these guides." This can save you a lot of time because it helps you identify just those Clearinghouse documents that contain the keyword or phrase you specify.

Clearinghouse guides to Internet job resources

Among the many subject guides available from the University of Michigan Clearinghouse, you'll find three that deal specifically with Internet job-search and employment-related features:

- *"Employment Opportunities and Job Resources on the Internet," by Margaret F. Riley of the Gordon Library at Worcester Polytechnic Institute in Worcester, Massachusetts. This is the most comprehensive of the three. It's organized by Internet feature (newsgroups, Telnet, Gopher, mailing lists, and World Wide Web) and is updated periodically to include additional services. (Clearinghouse filename: "jobs:riley")*

- *"Job Search and Employment Opportunities: Best Bets from the Net," by Philip Ray and Bradley Taylor of the University of Michigan. This guide takes a different approach. Rather than cover all the employment-related features and services on the Internet, Messrs. Ray and Taylor identify and describe only what they consider to be the "Best Bets" for job seekers in several broad areas—Education and Academe, Humanities and Social Science, Science and Technology, etc. The Net can be overwhelming, but this well-written and well-organized guide makes it seem almost manageable. (Clearinghouse filename: "employment:raytay")*

- *"Finding Library Jobs and Library Employment: Navigating and Electronic Web," by John Fenner of the University of Western*

> *Ontario, is a must-have file for anyone planning a job search for a traditional library position. Mr. Fenner, a graduate student himself, has assembled into a single 60-plus page document a wealth of information about newsgroups, mailing lists, Gophers, and other Internet resources of special interest to librarians or librarians-to-be. (Clearinghouse filename: "jobs:fenner")*

The Gopher Jewels!

The RiceInfo Gopher and the University of Michigan Clearinghouse are two of the three most important subject-oriented services on the Net. The third is a Gopher feature called *Gopher Jewels*. Created by the Gopher Jewels Project under the leadership of David Riggins, this feature celebrated its first birthday June 1, 1994.

The basic concept is simple: Collect the Gopher menus from many leading Gopher sites. Then go through them all, classifying each menu item by subject. When you're done, rearrange all the items into a new, master menu in which everything is presented by *subject*.

You will find the general structure of the Gopher Jewels menu system below. But, as an example, if you were to pick the second main item, "Community, Global, and Environmental," you would be taken to a menu offering items like the "1993 National Environmental Scorecard"; Global Warming; plus gateways to the EchoGopher and the GreenGopher at the University of Virginia, as well as the Great Lakes Information Network.

Contents of the Gopher Jewels

Like all Gophers, the Gopher Jewels menu comprises a powerful, easy-to-use, and incredibly seductive system. If you have one tenth of an ounce of curiosity in your body, you will find yourself signing on to research one topic and end up an hour later with a stack of printouts that have nothing to do with your original quest. Which is not only just fine, it's wonderful!

Here is the general layout of the Gopher Jewels menu system. Notice that everything is categorized by subject. (The slash at the end of some lines is the Gopher symbol meaning that particular item leads to another menu.)

```
                    CONTENTS OF GOPHER JEWELS
1. Gopher Jewels Information and Help/
      1. About Gopher Jewels.
      2. Gopher Help Documents/
      3. Gopher Jewels Announcement Archives/
      4. Gopher Jewels Discussion    Archives/
      5. Other Archives and Related Information/

2. Community, Global and Environmental/
      1. Country Specific Information/
      2. Environment/
      3. Free-Nets And Other Community Or State Gophers/
      4. Global or World-Wide Topics/

3. Education, Social Sciences, Arts & Humanities/
      1. Anthropology and Archaeology/
      2. Arts and Humanities/
      3. Education (Includes K-12)/
      4. Genealogy/
      5. Geography/
      6. History/
      7. Language/
      8. Religion and Philosophy/
      9. Social Science/

4. Economics, Business and Store Fronts/
      1. Economics and Business/
      2. Products and Services - Store Fronts/

5. Engineering and Industrial Applications/
      1. Architecture/
      2. Engineering Related/
      3. Manufacturing/
      4. Safety/

6. Government/
      1. Federal Agency and Related Gopher Sites/
      2. Military/
      3. Political and Government/
      4. State Government/

7. Health, Medical, and Disability/
      1. AIDS and HIV Information/
      2. Disability Information/
      3. Medical Related/
      4. Psychology/
```

8. Internet and Computer Related Resources/
      1. A List Of Gophers With Subject Trees/
      2. Computer Related/
      3. Internet Cyberspace related/
      4. Internet Resources by Type (Gopher, Phone, USENET, WAIS, Other)/
      5. Internet Service Providers/
      6. List of Lists Resources/

9. Law/
      1. Legal or Law related/
      2. Patents and Copyrights/

10. Library, Reference, and News/
      1. Books, Journals, Magazines, Newsletters, and Publications/
      2. General Reference Resources/
      3. Journalism/
      4. Library Information and Catalogs/
      5. News Related Services/
      6. Radio and TV Broadcasting/

11. Miscellaneous Items/

12. Natural Sciences including Mathematics/
      1. Agriculture and Forestry/
      2. Astronomy and Astrophysics/
      3. Biological Sciences/
      4. Chemistry/
      5. Geology and Oceanography/
      6. Math Sciences/
      7. Meteorology/
      8. Physics/

13. Personal Development and Recreation/
      1. Employment Opportunities and Resume Postings/
      2. Fun Stuff & Multimedia/
      3. Museums, Exhibits and Special Collections/
      4. Travel Information/

14. Research, Technology Transfer and Grants Opportunities/
      1. Grants/
      2. Technical Reports/
      3. Technology Transfer/

⇨ How to get to the Gopher Jewels

To reach the "Mother Site" of the Gopher Jewels, Gopher to **cwis.usc.edu** and choose "Other Gophers and Information Resources" and then "Gopher Jewels."

Once you reach the Mother Site, you will be able to get information on *mirror sites*, locations that duplicate the Mother Site but may be located closer to your location. By opting to use them instead of "Mother," you will help reduce Net traffic. At present, there are mirror sites in Australia, Great Britain, Israel, and Turkey.

Other World Wide Web (http) and Gopher URLs include:

➤ http://galaxy.einet.net/gopher/gopher.html

➤ http://galaxy.einet.net/GJ/index.html

➤ gopher://cwis.usc.edu/11/Other_Gophers_and_
Information_Resources/Gophers_by_Subject/Gopher_Jewels

➤ gopher://info.monash.edu.au/11/Other/sources/
Gopher_Jewels

➤ gopher://gopher.technion.ac.il/11/Other_gophers/
Gopher_Jewels

 # Library of Congress MARVEL Gopher

The United States Library of Congress has got to be one of the primary information sources in the entire world. And to its everlasting credit, in our experience over the past decade or so, it has vigorously pursued a goal of making its information and catalogues accessible by electronic means.

It thus comes as no surprise to find that the Library of Congress has a very strong and impressive presence on the Internet. But the key thing to remember is that the Library of Congress (LC) MARVEL Gopher is not limited to just books and other Library of Congress resources. Far from it. The design philosophy of the LC MARVEL Gopher is to get you plugged into the Net *by subject*. So you will find that this Gopher may be but a starting point from which you will be taken to other Gophers and resources.

To get to the Library of Congress Gopher, check first for references to "LC MARVEL" on the Gopher menus of your access provider if they offer such. If not, opt for "All the Gophers in the World" or otherwise get into a position where you can specify a given Gopher address. When prompted, Gopher to **marvel.loc.gov** and use Port 70 if you find you must. Or try Telnetting to the location **marvel.loc.gov** and logging in as "marvel." (Using Gopher access is recommended, however, because there are only 15 Telnet ports.)

You will see a menu that looks like the one shown here. Choose Item 10, "Global Electronic Library...," to display the subject-matter menu:

```
Library of Congress MARVEL Gopher
Page 1 of 1

1    About LC MARVEL                                       Menu
2    Events, Facilities, Publications, and Services        Menu
3    Research and Reference (Public Services)              Menu
4    Libraries and Publishers (Technical Services)         Menu
5    Copyright                                             Menu
6    Library of Congress Online Systems                    Menu
7    Employee Information                                  Menu
8    U.S. Congress                                         Menu
9    Government Information                                 Menu
10   Global Electronic Library (by Subject)                Menu
11   Internet Resources                                    Menu
12   What's New on LC MARVEL                               Menu
13   Search LC MARVEL Menus                                Menu

Enter Item Number, SAVE, ?, or BACK: 10

Global Electronic Library (by Subject)
Page 1 of 1

1    About this menu                          Text
2    Reference                                Menu
3    Library Science                          Menu
4    Philosophy and Religion                  Menu
5    Language, Linguistics, and Literature    Menu
6    The Arts                                 Menu
7    Social Sciences                          Menu
8    Law                                      Menu
9    Economics and Business                   Menu
10   History and Geography                    Menu
11   Medicine and Psychology                  Menu
12   Natural Science                          Menu
13   Mathematics                              Menu
14   Applied Science and Technology           Menu
15   Sports and Recreation                    Menu

Enter Item Number, SAVE, ?, or BACK:
```

The menus and submenus offered by the LC MARVEL Gopher will keep an information junkie busy (and supremely content) for days and days. In our opinion, even though your main focus right now is landing a job, you owe it to yourself to spend an evening exploring this resource. Just to bring yourself up to speed on what's out there. And who knows, one or two of the things you find just might prove to be an interesting (and impressive) topic you can discuss with an interviewer.

 # Conclusion

Our recommendation to take some time to simply explore applies to all of the resources and sites we've highlighted here. They are truly among the best that the Internet has to offer. And we feel very strongly that it's important to identify the best.

For the Internet is a vast, rolling tide, under which one can easily drown. We want to keep you afloat, of course. But we also want to help you bend the tides of information to your will. The chapters presented in Part 1 have gotten you quickly up to speed on hardware, software, and Internet basics. They have introduced essential tools and concepts and shown you how to use the Net in general.

In Part 2 of this book, we will help you zero in on *specific* job-search features. But we're going to begin with a chapter on the employment-oriented features available on such "non-Internet" systems as CompuServe, Prodigy, and America Online. Certainly there is a distinction between the Internet and the world of commercial, consumer-oriented systems. But when you're looking for a job, you want to cast your net as wide as possible. And many of the features on these systems are so good that we would all be foolish to ignore them.

Part 2

Career
explorations

Non-Internet options

America Online, CompuServe, & Prodigy

CHAPTER 6

NON-INTERNET options? You have a right to be surprised. After all, we've just spent most of the first part of this book getting you connected and up to speed on the Internet. Why pause now to talk about the special employment-related features offered by America Online, CompuServe, and Prodigy?

The answer is that "Job seekers cannot live by Internet alone." Well, they can, actually. But it would be foolish for anyone to completely ignore the three leading commercial online systems and the millions of people who use them, particularly since you may very well be using one of these systems as your means of connecting to the Internet.

Let us be as clear as we can be. As you know from Chapter 2, we feel that America Online and Delphi currently offer most readers the easiest, least expensive way to access the Internet. But Internet access and features are *not* what we're talking about here. The focus of this chapter is non-Internet online features that are likely to be of interest to any job seeker with a computer and a modem.

That means that Delphi is off the board, because it offers virtually nothing specifically tailored to job seekers. As for GEnie, its only exclusive employment-related feature is the Dr. Job question-and-answer column. Good as it may be, Dr. Job is hardly reason enough to open an account on GEnie.

So, at this writing, the quest for non-Internet, job-related features on the leading commercial online systems comes down to the Big Three—America Online, CompuServe, and Prodigy.

Cost, convenience, & coherence

The biggest drawback to these three systems is the cost. As you know from Chapter 2, you can expect to pay about $10 a month for a subscription that gives you unlimited access to a package of 100 or more basic services. But if you venture beyond those basic services, you can spend quite a bit more indeed.

Is it worth it? Is it worth 25 cents a minute to be able to instantly search through tens of thousands of articles from leading business magazines and newsletters published over the last ten years? Is it worth 40 cents a minute to be able to search the *Harvard Business Review*, *Books in Print*, or Standard & Poor's for companies, people, and subjects that might bear on your job search?

We think so. In fact, these prices are an incredible bargain. And when you consider that it is your career and your future that are at stake, they are truly cheap at the price. After all, while none of us would be happy about spending $15 to get the information we needed to do a term paper or homework assignment, when it comes to a job search, $15 is nothing.

Better organized than the Net

America Online, CompuServe, and Prodigy have some really wonderful things to offer. The fact that you will have to pay a bit extra to take advantage of them is actually a good thing. These systems and the providers of these extra-value features are in business to make a profit. Consequently their offerings tend to be much more convenient to use and much better organized than all the "free" features on the Internet. That saves you time and trouble, and, assuming your time has value, it can save you money.

There's also the fact that if you are having trouble or have a question—or if you simply are not satisfied with the level of service—there's someone you can *complain* to. This is definitely *not* the case on the Internet.

In this chapter, we'll introduce you to the non-Internet employment-related features on America Online, CompuServe, and Prodigy. But we'll start with one of the most important skills of all—getting an *index* of your chosen system's features.

 # Searching the index

Online systems have so many features that it can be difficult to keep track of all that's available. That's why the single most important technique you can learn for using any system is how to get an *index* or a list of system *keywords*.

Each of the Big Three will let you search for features of interest while you are online, and you will definitely want to do so. But you will also want to capture a system's complete list of keywords in a file on disk. That way you can use your word processing software to print it out or to search it at your leisure.

Here is what to do on each system.

✳ America Online keywords

To search the system's keyword list, click on the "Go To" menu and mouse down to Directory of Services. Or click on the Flash Bar icon showing a magnifying glass looking at a disk to "Search Directory of Services." Then just respond to the prompt for a search word or phrase.

On AOL, you can key in Ctrl-K (hold down your Ctrl key and hit K) to get a prompt for a keyword you want to enter to be taken instantly to some feature. The Directory of Services includes the keyword needed to reach any given feature instantly.

To capture a list of all AOL keywords in a file, use the keyword "help" to get to the Help feature. Then click on "Members' Online Support." And then click on "Using Keywords to Get Around." You will be able to tell the system to display all the keywords associated with each major area. After a list has been displayed, click on "File" and then "Save As" to be prompted for the name of the file you want to use.

✳ CompuServe "Go" words

Key in go index or use whatever your software offers regarding getting a current index of the system. (At last count, there were at

least 20 different programs designed to give you an interface to the CompuServe system.) When you get to the CompuServe Index page, you'll be able to search on the basis of a keyword (like "jobs" or "employment"). You can also request the entire index. So tell your software to open a capture file, and then request the full index. Close the capture file and you're done.

✳ Prodigy "Jump" words

Click on the "A-Z" tool at the bottom of the screen. Then search for keywords of interest. On Prodigy, you can enter Ctrl-J (hold down your Ctrl key and hit J) to get a prompt for a "jump" word that will instantly take you to a desired part of the system.

Capturing Prodigy's complete list of keywords is not easy. You must first click on T for "tools" and set your print options so that everything that would normally go to the printer ends up in a disk file. Then you click on the "A-Z" button to get to the index, and then you must click on "Pr" to print. Prodigy will ask you to specify the range of pages you want to print. When you do so, the system will probably warn you that this will take some time. It does, indeed. Expect to spend at least 15 minutes on this process.

 # America Online jobs features

As you know from Chapter 2, America Online provides a handsome, easy-to-use graphical interface. That's why, for many people, AOL is the provider of choice for Internet access. But leave all that aside for the time being and instead, search the AOL Directory of Services on the keyword "job." You will see a screen like the one shown in Fig. 6-1.

Notice that there are nine offerings. As we are about to see, the first item on the list, the Career Center, is the mother lode that embraces nearly all the other items on this list. The last two items, Casa Blanca Works and Peachtree Software, are what information professionals call "false drops." They contain the search word but have nothing to do with the goal of the search. Casa Blanca Works has a product that will "display the job queue at each printer," and Peachtree Software offers a "job costing" package.

Figure 6-1

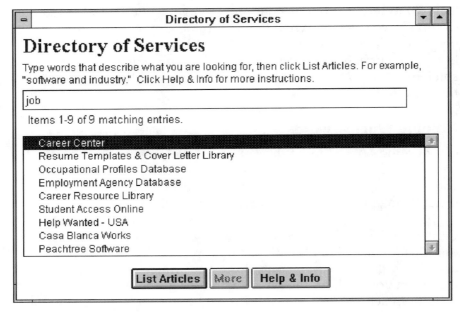

You can search America Online's Directory of Services for job-related features using the keyword "job."

The only other item on this list that is not covered by the Career Center is Student Access Online. This is a service of the test-preparation coaching firm, the Princeton Review. It pulls together a number of resources to help you get more out of college, expand your graduate school and career options, and put you in touch with students nationwide. You can reach this feature directly using the keyword "student."

 # James Gonyea's AOL Career Center

James C. Gonyea, president of Gonyea and Associates, Inc., has had over 22 years of experience offering career and employment guidance, career planning, and job placement services. He is the author of at least six books, including *The On-Line Job Search Companion* from McGraw-Hill.

In 1989, Mr. Gonyea created the nation's first electronic career and employment guidance service, the Career Center, and offered it on America Online. The Career Center has grown considerably since then. Indeed, as we will see in the next chapter, Mr. Gonyea is now one of the leading providers of job and employment information on the Internet. This leads to a bit of confusion about names. The Career Center on America Online and the Online Career Center (OCC) on the Internet are two *separate* entities, although they both offer some of the same resources.

You will find the Career Center in the Learning & Reference department of AOL. Or you can go there immediately using the keyword "career." When you do, you will see a screen like the one shown in Fig. 6-2.

Figure 6-2

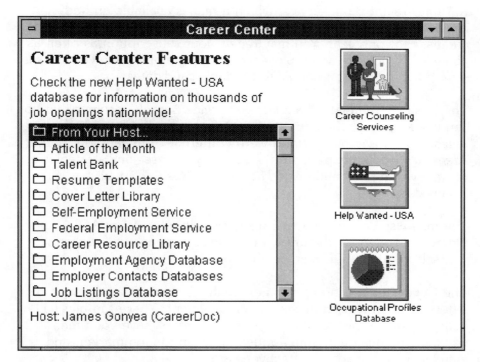

AOL Career Center's main menu.

You will definitely want to click on the "From Your Host" item at the top of the menu the first time you use this feature. This will display a letter from Mr. Gonyea designed to give you a quick overview of all the features offered by the Career Center.

The "Article of the Month" selection leads to one or more articles written by Gonyea and Associates. These tend to be career guidance-style articles designed to alert you to the need for self-assessment, goal setting, follow-up, and so on.

 # The Talent Bank, Resumes, & Letters

The next item is the Talent Bank. At a cost of $40 a year, Gonyea and Associates will put your resume into its Worldwide Resume/Talent Bank service, which it makes available on both America Online and on the Internet. Your resume will remain in the database for one year. You may renew your subscription as often as you wish. If you are an employer looking for employees, you can also search the Talent Bank on AOL for likely candidates.

The Resume Templates area lets you review sample resumes that you can use as guides when attempting to write or edit your own resume. Twelve of the sample resumes were written by Tom Jackson, one of America's leading experts on the subject of job-seeking strategies and resume writing and author of *The Perfect Resume*, published by Doubleday, Inc.

You may also download actual resumes written by other AOL members, and upload your own resume as a means of "marketing" yourself to other AOL members nationwide.

The Cover Letter Library, the next feature, contains a collection of letters commonly used in seeking employment. These samples will help you shape the wording of your own letters, save you time, enhance the quality of your "appearance" in the job market, and increase your job search effectiveness.

The letters were written by James Gonyea, and they cover everything from submitting your application to confirming an interview appointment to formally accepting an offer of employment.

Self-Employment & Federal Employment

The Self-Employment Service is designed to help you select a self-employment direction, as well as to provide guidance and information to assist you in starting and operating a successful business. The major emphasis at this writing is on helping people start a "home-based" business, especially businesses that involve the use of a personal computer.

The Self-Employment service gives you access to dozens of profiles of people who are operating successful home-based, computer-assisted businesses. A number of "turnkey" business service kits which promise to help you "instantly" set up such a business are offered for sale from the Career Center. These include an Apartment Matching/Referral Service, an Educational/Career Consulting Service, and a Professional Billing Service. Additional business opportunities will be added on a regular basis.

The Federal Employment Service (FES) is a collection of information about federal employment opportunities compiled by the New England Center for Career Development. The purpose of FES is to provide you with extensive information regarding how to seek and secure employment with the federal government.

Within this collection of information, you will find detailed information on 162 of the most common and important federal departments and agencies.

The Career Resource Library

The Career Resource Library is the main location within the Career Center where you can find additional resources (not currently

available in the Career Center or elsewhere on America Online) that can help you satisfy your career development needs. The Library was designed to be your "next step" if the resources you need are not available online.

The items found listed in the Library come in a variety of formats, including everything from audiocassettes and books to CD-ROMs and software packages, films, newsletters, videotapes, workshops, and seminars. (Much of the information found in the Library is supplied by JIST Works, Inc., a nationally recognized leader in the publishing industry of career and employment resources.)

 # Employment Agency & Employer Contacts Databases

The menu item "Employment Agency Database" takes you to the Executive Search Firms area. Here you will find information on thousands of professional executive search firms, recruitment agencies, headhunters, placement agencies, and the like that may be able to assist you in finding a job.

The information used to create the Executive Search Firm area has been obtained from two main sources. One source is Custom Databanks, Inc., of Georgetown, Maryland. Custom Databanks specializes in the collection and distribution of information on executive search firms. They have supplied the Career Center with information on 4,000 search firms. This information can be found by selecting the "Search Custom Databanks Database" menu item.

Another source is the executive search firms themselves. They place profiles of their agencies in this area as a means of marketing their services. These profiles can be found in the "Search Recruiters Plus Database" area. The number of agencies found in this database changes as new profiles are uploaded.

The next item, "Employer Contacts Databases," is a collection of informative profiles of several thousand American employers. The purpose of this collection is to assist you in your job search by

helping you find potential employers whose needs are likely to match your skills and experience.

The Employer Contacts service is comprised of information supplied by Demand Research Corporation in Columbus, Ohio. Demand Research publishes and distributes a database that contains information on every one of the approximately 6,000 U.S. public companies that are listed on the New York Stock Exchange, the American Stock Exchange, and the NASDAQ National Market System.

The database is updated daily and is available for sale to businesses, organizations, and individuals wishing to own a copy for their own use. For more information on obtaining a copy of the database, see the menu item labeled "Ordering The Executive Desk Register" on the Employer Contacts menu.

Job Listings Database

The final item shown on the boxed menu in Fig. 6-2 is "Job Listings Database." In this area, you will find three services designed to help you find employment opportunities: Help Wanted-USA, the E-Span employment database, and the Classifieds Bulletin Board.

✳ Help Wanted-USA

A product of Gonyea and Associates, Help Wanted-USA claims to be the largest electronic source of employment ads available on any commercial computer online network service. "On average, you can expect to find 6000+ job opening announcements each week," according to the company.

Occupations are professional in nature, cover most career fields, and represent companies nationwide. Employment listings are collected by private consultants in cities nationwide and electronically uploaded to the Career Center. This database is updated weekly, usually late on Tuesday or early Wednesday morning.

Employers who wish to learn how to advertise their help wanted notices in the Help Wanted-USA database may call Gonyea and Associates at 813-372-1333 (Florida); request information via e-mail (use the AOL screen name "CareerDoc"); or fax a request to 813-372-0394.

As we will see in Chapter 6, Help Wanted-USA can be searched on the Internet using a Gopher menu. It is also available on the World Wide Web. But its Web implementation leaves much to be desired. In our opinion, the easiest, most satisfying way to search Help Wanted-USA is via AOL's Career Center.

✳ E-Span

Like Help Wanted-USA, the E-Span database contains information about employment openings in various career fields from companies nationwide. The majority of these listings are unique to E-Span and are not available to the general public. This database is updated *every* week, usually on Monday. Employment listings for the database are supplied by E-Span.

Employers wishing to advertise their help wanted notices in the E-Span database may do so by contacting E-Span directly at 8440 Woodfield Crossing, Suite 170, Indianapolis, IN 46240, or by calling 800-682-2901.

The Help Wanted-USA and E-Span databases offer America Online members a quick and easy means of finding employment opportunities. You may use both databases to locate a new job, or keep abreast of the employment market in your career field or area of interest. There are no charges (other than connect charges) to view these listings. To view the actual employment listings, select the items "Search the Help Wanted-USA database" or "Search E-Span database" from the Job Listing menu.

✳ The Classifieds Bulletin Board

If you wish to view help wanted ads that other America Online members have posted, or if you wish to post your own help wanted ad (outside of the Help Wanted-USA and E-Span area), check out the

Classifieds Bulletin Board area in the Travel & Shopping department. There you may browse through ads or place an ad yourself. Remember, though, the number of online members viewing the Help Wanted-USA and E-Span databases is almost certain to be substantially higher than those viewing the Classified listings.

Career Counseling Services

Finally, notice that the Career Center screen offers three large buttons called Career Counseling Services, Help Wanted-USA, and Occupational Profiles Database. (The Help Wanted button just gets you to that feature faster than clicking on the Job Listings Database selection.)

Jim Gonyea's Career Center offers extensive career counseling services. Three main services are involved: Career Counseling, Career Focus 2000, and the Career Analysis Service.

✳ Career counseling

You are invited to meet online in a group counseling session with an experienced, professional career counselor to discuss your career needs and problems. Counseling is available by signing up for a group counseling session. To do so, refer to the Appointment Book in the Career Counseling section of the Career Center. If you are experiencing difficulty in selecting a career direction, career counseling is usually recommended *after* you have completed one of the other two career guidance options (Career Focus 2000 or Career Analysis Services).

There is no fee for the counseling service other than your normal America Online fees.

✳ Career Focus 2000

This service consists of a series of four "workbook" exercises that you may download and complete at your leisure. The heart of the program is an interest inventory (Booklets 1 and 2) that allows you to sample 225 work activities and then compare your strongest interests to approximately 1,000 occupations as a means of finding those that

match your interests. Booklet 3 guides you in selecting a specific career goal, and Booklet 4 helps you develop a plan to reach your career goal. There is no charge for the use of the Career Focus 2000 materials.

✳ Career Analysis Service

This is a comprehensive, computer-assisted analysis service designed to identify occupations that match your interests, abilities, and work preferences. This service is appropriate for individuals who wish a more thorough analysis of career options than what is possible with the Career Focus 2000 program.

You first download and complete a questionnaire indicating your preference for various work activities, abilities, and work situations. You then e-mail your answers back to the Career Center. A professional career counselor will then enter your answers into an occupational database and compare them to over 13,500 occupations. Within one week, you will receive via e-mail a listing of occupations (by job title) which best match your interests, abilities, and work preferences. There is a one-time charge of $39.95 for use of the Career Analysis Service.

Occupational Profiles Database

This feature offers you extensive information on the kind of work, the level of pay, the promotion prospects, and just about any other bit of information you might need in order to get a clearer understanding of a given job, profession, or occupation.

There are some 800 profiles in all, and you can search the entire database by keyword. When we searched on "technical," for example, one of the many occupations that appeared was "Writer/Editor." The profile of that occupation went on for pages. Most impressive.

 # Chicago Tribune Help Wanted on AOL

In recent years there has been a headlong rush on the part of newspapers and magazines to get online. AOL thus offers not only *Time* magazine but also selected articles from the *New York Times*. You will also find the *Chicago Tribune*, which, unlike many other papers, includes its classified ad section.

Use the keyword "Chicago" to go to the Chicago Online feature shown in Fig. 6-3. Then select the *Chicago Tribune* feature, opt for Classifieds, and then click on the "Help Wanted" button. That will take you to a screen like the one shown in Fig. 6-4. Notice that here we have searched on the keyword "advertising." We clicked on the second item ("01/13:ADVERTISING Assistant needed full-time for small ad . . .") and the screen shown in Fig. 6-5 appeared.

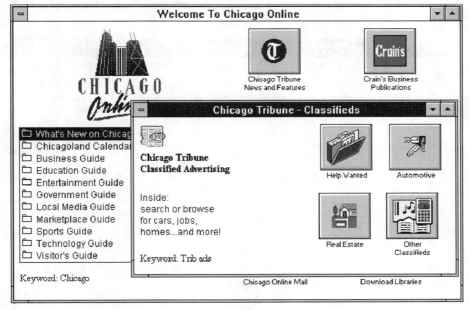

Figure 6-3

AOL's Chicago Online feature.

Figure 6-4

Searching the Chicago Tribune *classifieds for advertising positions resulted in 98 "hits."*

Figure 6-5

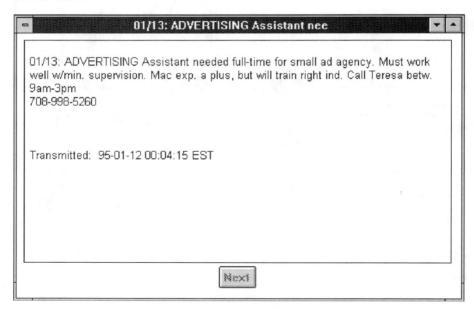

A sample job listing from the Chicago Tribune *classifieds.*

CompuServe job features

No one in the online world contests the fact that the CompuServe Information Service (CIS) is much broader and much deeper in its offerings than either America Online or Prodigy. Yet, at this writing, CompuServe has nothing to rival the Career Center on AOL.

For example, here is what a search of the CIS index on the keywords "job" and "employment" turned up:

```
Business Database Plus($)        BUSDB
Classifieds                      CLASSIFIEDS
E-Span Online Job Listing        ESPAN
FORTUNE                          FORTUNE
Government Giveaways Forum +      INFOUSA
IQuest($)                        IQUEST
Knowledge Index($)               KI
U.S. News & World Report         USNEWS
Warren, Gorham, Lamont. Auer.    WGL
Working-From-Home Forum +        WORK
```

The only item on this list that is directly job-related is, of course, the E-Span Online Job Listing feature. And, as we know, that is also available in the AOL Career Center, along with Help Wanted-USA. The Classifieds on CompuServe are a possibility, but this is not a heavy-duty job-finding feature.

Still, CompuServe should not be counted out as a job-finding resource. For, while it may not include vast lists of open positions, it does include some of the most powerful information retrieval tools you will find anywhere. Business Database Plus, for example, gives you access to the full text of five years' worth of over 500 business magazines. IQuest gives you access to literally hundreds of databases, each of which, in turn, includes hundreds of magazines and newsletters. And the Knowledge Index gives you low-cost, after-hours access to over 125 Dialog databases, including Standard & Poor's.

CompuServe, in short, should be viewed as a *research* tool. Later in this book we'll have much more to say about how researching a company online using CompuServe and other services can give you a leg up in your job quest.

97

 # Prodigy job features

At this writing, Prodigy offers two main job-related features. These are the Prodigy Classifieds and the Career Bulletin Board.

To sample the first feature, use the jump word "career opportunities." That will take you to a screen like the one shown in Fig. 6-6, the Online Classifieds. Click on the "Read/Place" button and you will see a screen like the one shown in Fig. 6-7. Notice that the fourth category is "Help Wanted." Click on that, and you will see a screen like the one shown in Fig. 6-8.

Although we could have searched the ad listings, we chose to click on "US Advertising Dir.," the fifth item in Fig. 6-8. That produced Fig. 6-9.

Figure 6-6

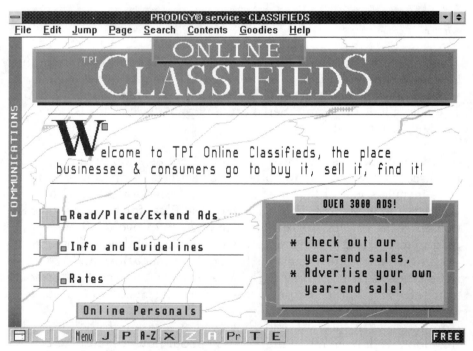

Prodigy's Online Classifieds opening screen.

Figure 6-7

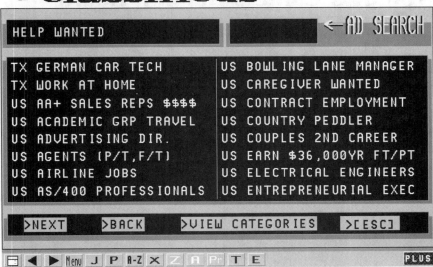

"Help Wanted" is one of several categories in Prodigy's classified ads.

Figure 6-8

Some sample listings of available jobs on Prodigy.

Figure 6-9

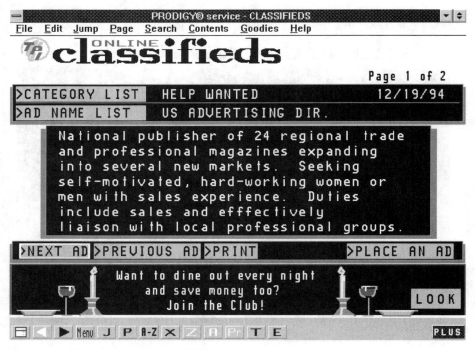

We located this brief description of a position for an Advertising Director.

Prodigy's Careers Bulletin Board

Certainly Prodigy's Online Classifieds are of interest and not to be overlooked by anyone who subscribes to the service. But this is not a heavy-duty job-finding feature. That's why you will also want to jump to "careers bb" to get to the Careers Bulletin Board.

Figure 6-10 shows the opening screen, overlaid with our request that Prodigy display the Topic List of the messages that have been posted to the board. Once again, this is not a heavy-duty job-finding feature, but at least it's something.

Figure 6-10

The opening screen for Prodigy's Careers Bulletin Board.

 # Conclusion

Authorities may differ on precise numbers. But clearly, there are tens of millions of Internet users, compared to the one to two million people who subscribe to each of the Big Three—America Online, CompuServe, and Prodigy. But the same limitations apply to all systems. Whether there are 20 million people with nominal access to a system or 2 million people who pay a monthly fee to have access, only a small percentage are going to check into a jobs-oriented feature.

But you cannot afford to leave any stone unturned. Therefore, in addition to taking advantage of strictly Internet features, it just makes good sense to post your resume to services like Help Wanted-USA,

E-Span, and similar offerings that are available on the Internet and on AOL, CompuServe, and Prodigy.

And, if jobs, career planning, and employment are your primary interest, the evidence points strongly in favor of getting yourself an America Online account. You may have heard it before, but at this writing, America Online offers the best interface to the Internet and, as we've seen here, the most extensive career- and jobs-oriented package of services.

Again, at this writing, the only primary Internet feature AOL does not yet offer is access to the World Wide Web. But this feature has been promised by means of a "coming soon" button on the AOL Internet access center. (And, as you will see when it arrives, the Web is a lot less than it has been cracked up to be.)

Prodigy, Delphi, and GEnie have some very nice features. But if you are primarily interested in using the online world to help you conduct a job search, then America Online and CompuServe are the systems of choice—America Online for its in-depth Career Center features an easy-to-use interface to the Internet, and CompuServe for its incredible information resources that you will want to use when developing information on a company, an industry, or even the person who may be interviewing you.

The Online
Career Center

WHEN it comes to finding a job, there is no magic bullet. There is no single action you can take that will guarantee your success and land you the job of your dreams. That's why we would be the last to suggest that you devote all your energies to the Internet/online approach. There is just no way to know whether your online efforts will pay off. At the same time, the easy availability of the Internet resources we'll show you how to use will definitely give you a leg up.

If you are already on CompuServe, America Online, or Prodigy, by all means tap into the features discussed in Chapter 6. But as we turn our attention to the Internet proper, two leading employment-related features come into view. The first is the Online Career Center (OCC), and the second is E-Span's Interactive Employment Network. We'll look at OCC in this chapter and at E-Span in Chapter 8.

 # The Online Career Center (OCC)

The Online Career Center is a nonprofit employer association located in Ann Arbor, Michigan. The job opportunities presented tend to favor high-tech positions, although real opportunities exist in other fields as well. You can submit an ASCII (plain text) version of your resume at no charge.

Your resume will remain on the system for 90 days. All expenses are paid by OCC member employers, companies that pay an annual fee to post their job openings with the service. You can search this list of job openings by job title, keyword, company name, or geographical region.

You can Gopher directly to **occ.com** and select "Online Career Center." Or use your Web browser to specify the URL **http://www.occ.com/occ/**. This will produce a screen like the one shown in Fig. 7-1.

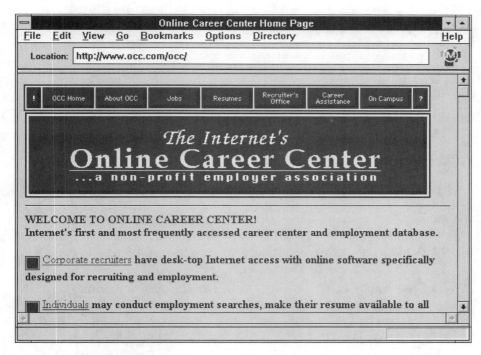

Figure 7-1

The Internet's Online Career Center.

 # OCC by Gopher

As you know, we acknowledge that the World Wide Web is really quite pretty. But when it's pure text-based information you are after, the Web is a real waste of time. So, too, for that matter, is America Online and any other "graphical" interface. Thus, in preparing this chapter, we opted for the plain (fast) text of Delphi.

We used Delphi to Gopher to **occ.com** and here is the opening menu we saw:

```
Online Career Center
Page 1 of 1

1  * Search Jobs                                  Menu
2  * Search Resumes                               Menu
3  1994 College & University Resume Books/Diskettes  Menu
4  About Online Career Center                     Menu
```

```
 5  Career Assistance                               Menu
 6  Company Sponsors and Profiles                   Menu
 7  Employment Events                               Menu
 8  FAQ - Frequently Asked Questions about OCC      Menu
 9  Help Files: Keyword Search/Enter Resume/Print   Menu
10  How To Enter A Resume                           Text
11  Online Career Center - On Campus                Menu
12  Online Career Center Liability Policy           Text
13  Questions and Comments to: occ@iquest.net       Text
14  Recruitment Advertising Agencies                Menu

Enter Item Number, SAVE, ?, or BACK:
```

How to post your resume on OCC

You may—at no cost—enter your full-text resume into the OCC Internet database via e-mail. Here's what to do:

- *Prepare your resume as pure, plain ASCII text, limiting your lines to no more than 70 characters.*

- *Send your resume via e-mail to **occ-resumes@occ.com**. Be sure to send it as part of your message, not as an "attached" or "encoded" file. In other words, make sure you can actually see it within the body of your message before sending it to OCC.*

- *Keep in mind that the "Subject:" line in your e-mail message serves as your resume "title." That means it will be the first information seen by employers when viewing your resume. So don't put your name on the "Subject:" line. Employers prefer to see something like "Accountant/CPA 5 Yrs Exp—Will Relocate."*

- *Your resume will stay in the OCC database for 90 days. To extend the time period beyond 90 days, simply re-enter it. Similarly, if you want to update or make changes to your resume, submit the new version and the previous one will disappear. (Each e-mail account number is permitted only one resume at a time in the database.)*

- *If you don't have Internet access, you can mail your typed resume (cover letter optional) to:*

Online Resume Service
1713 Hemlock Lane
Plainfield, IN 46168-1830

Your typewritten resume will be processed and entered online into the OCC resume database for six months. Each resume submitted to

Online Resume Service must contain a "title line" not to exceed 45 spaces. For example: "Chemical Engr/5 Yrs Exp/Oil Industry-NY."

The cost for this service is $10.00 for resumes up to three pages in length. Checks or money orders should be made payable to Online Resume Service.

A service broad & deep

Whether you're searching for a job or for qualified employees, it's difficult to avoid feeling that you've hit the jackpot when you look at the OCC menu—it's quite rich with features and information. We'll hit the highlights here, but we encourage you to sign on and explore on your own.

Be warned, however, that in our experience, the OCC system is often busy and unable to admit even one more person. That may change as OCC adds more equipment and access lines, but it can be frustrating. The only remedy at this writing is persistence.

Searching for a job

Searching for a job on the Online Career Center is clearly the main event. Once again, you can do so using a text-based system like Delphi or a graphical World Wide Web browser like Mosaic, Netscape, NetCruiser, or some other piece of software. Indeed, you can use a Web browser to access the OCC Gopher as a URL.

In our experience, however, tapping into a system like OCC in pure, plain text mode is not only faster, but much more convenient. Without exception, your Web browser software will let you capture everything that appears on your screen as a file on disk. But that file will be an HTML file, with all the hypertext markup language codes in place. You can strip those codes out to create a plain text file using a utility like DE-HTML once you are offline.

But why bother? You can get the identical information much faster— and with no need for post-session processing—if you simply sign

onto a text-based system like Delphi, open your comm program's capture buffer to record all incoming text to disk, and plunge into the Online Career Center.

Opening your capture buffer to record everything to a file is like turning on a camcorder. You won't miss anything. But you will want to edit the resulting "videotape" and clip out the really good stuff once you are offline. That's easy to do.

Just close your capture buffer and leave your comm program. Then bring the capture file into your favorite word processor. Use your word processor's *search* or *find* function to locate text of interest. Then clip it out and copy it to another file. When you've extracted all the goodies, you can simply delete the capture file.

Regardless of your means of access, when you select the first item, "* Search Jobs," from the main OCC menu, you will see something like this:

```
* Search Jobs
Page 1 of 1

1  * Browse Jobs:      Jobs By City          Menu
2  * Browse Jobs:      Jobs By Company       Menu
3  * Browse Jobs:      Jobs By State         Menu
4  * International:    International Jobs     Search
5  * Keyword Search:   Contract Jobs<?>      Search
6  * Keyword Search:   Search All Jobs<?>    Search
7  Canada:            All Provinces          Search
8  East:              DE/MD/NJ/PA/VA/WV/DC   Search
9  Midwest:           IL/IN/KS/KY/MI/OH/WI   Search
10 North Central:     IA/MN/NE/ND/SD         Search
11 Northeast:         CT/ME/MA/NH/NY/RI/VT   Search
12 Northwest:         AK/ID/MT/OR/WA/WY      Search
13 South Central:     AR/LA/MO/OK/TX         Search
14 South:             AL/FL/GA/MS/NC/SC/TN   Search
15 West:              AZ/CA/CO/HI/NV/NM/UT   Search

Enter Item Number, SAVE, ?, or BACK:
```

 # Searching by location

At this point, things become quite obvious and intuitive. If you select the first item, you will be presented with a menu of cities ranging from Albuquerque, New Mexico, to Tokyo, Japan. Pick a city from

that menu, and you will be shown a menu listing all of the jobs in the OCC database that are located there. When we chose "Philadelphia," for example, we got a menu listing 167 jobs that looked like this:

```
Philadelphia, Pennsylvania
Page 1 of 1

1  [Jan 09] Philadelphia PA HIGH LEVEL Designer              Text
2  [Jan 07] Part-Time Philly User-Interface PC Windows C/C++  Text
3  [Jan 05] UNISYS NETWORKING SUPPORT                         Text
4  [Jan 04] Copywriter / Proofreader (PA)                     Text
5  [Jan 04] Creative Caterer 2000 (PA)                        Text
6  [Jan 04] Dental Claim Reviewer (PA)                        Text
7  [Jan 04] Garment Specification Inspector (PA)              Text
8  [Jan 04] Group Psychotherapist (PA)                        Text
9  [Jan 04] Home Care Health Attendent (PA)                   Text
10 [Jan 04] Librarian / Cataloger (PA)                        Text
11 [Jan 04] Licensed Practical Nurse (PA)                     Text
12 [Jan 04] Managing Editor (PA)                              Text
13 [Jan 04] Marketing (PA)                                    Text
14 [Jan 04] Marketing Director - Bicycling Magazine (PA)      Text
15 [Jan 04] Meat Cutter (PA)                                  Text
16 [Jan 04] Medical Assistant (PA)                            Text
17 [Jan 04] Nurse Case Manager (NJ)                           Text
18 [Jan 04] Programmer / Analyst (PA)                         Text
19 [Jan 04] Purchaser (PA)                                    Text
20 [Jan 04] Quality Assurance Representatives (PA)            Text
21 [Jan 04] Quality Control Supervisor (PA)                   Text
22 [Jan 04] Registered Nurse (PA)                             Text
23 [Jan 04] Registered Nurse (PA)                             Text
24 [Jan 04] School Psychologist (PA)                          Text
25 [Jan 04] Social Worker (PA)                                Text
   .
   .
   .
(etc.)
```

 # The keyword connection

We are in *love* with database software and the power that it gives people over the information in their lives—whether it's an address book or household inventory or financial, investment, and tax records. And we have had this love affair ever since writing the instruction manual for a commercial database package designed for the Tandy Radio Shack TRS-80 back in the early 1980s.

A properly structured database lets you slice and dice information any way you please. It also lets you *find* information on the basis of one or more keywords. And that's exactly what the Online Career Center's keyword search feature is all about.

As we have seen, if the location of your next job is the main concern, OCC makes it easy to come up with a list of possibilities, almost regardless of the state or city you want. But if the work itself is paramount, you can use the OCC keyword search feature to find all the listings for a job of a particular kind.

This can be a powerful feature. Just be aware that not everyone thinks alike. So what might be an obvious keyword to you may not appear in some of the job listings you would like to see, simply because the person who prepared the listing did not think to include your "obvious" keyword. So be creative. Experiment. And be patient.

Fortunately, there aren't many obvious words for the kind of work we do. So when we used this feature to search for all jobs for a *writer*, OCC responded with a list of more than 80 items. An abbreviated version of the menu that appeared is shown here:

```
Search for: writer
* Keyword Search: Search All Jobs<?>
Page 1 of 1

1  [Jan 25] Technical Writer (TX)                              Text
2  [Jan 25] Brokerage Producers (U)                            Text
3  [Jan 25] Technical Documentation Writer (CA)                Text
4  [Jan 20] US-CA-Sunnyvale/Tech Writer/Contract/Recruiter     Text
5  [Jan 20] UK London - HTML Writer/designer                   Text
6  [Jan 17] Presales Support/Technical Proposal Writer (PA)    Text
7  [Jan 17] Commercial Insurance Sales - Producer (U )         Text
8  [Jan 17] Technical Marketing Writer (DE)                    Text
9  [Jan 17] Technical Writer (TN)                              Text
10 [Jan 17] US-VA-Reston Technical Writer                      Text
11 [Jan 17] US-MA-Boston Software Tech Writer Contract         Text
12 [Jan 17] Montreal Technical Writer                          Text
13 [Jan 09] Grant Writer Needed                                Text
14 [Jan 05] PA - Technical Writer - Diebold (Medselect)        Text
15 [Jan 05] Nationwide-Programmer/Analysts & Database Admin -  Text
16 [Dec 27] CO COBOL/MVS/DATACOM/UNIX/ORACLE/C++ TSSI          Text
17 [Dec 20] Senior_Technical_Writer                            Text
18 [Dec 20] Internal_Tools                                     Text
19 [Dec 20] Technical_Writer                                   Text
20 [Dec 20] Editor-Writer                                      Text
```

```
21 [Dec 15] CO - Marketing Writer - JD Edwards & Company       Text
.
.
.
(etc.)
```

⇨ Here's a job listing

As you would expect, the writing jobs that were presented as part of the "Philadelphia" listing we looked at earlier showed up here as well. As did many others. What we found surprising was that many of the entries on the "Writer" menu were for the identical jobs. A job listed on the menu as "Technical Writer" might also appear as a separate listing as "Writer—Delaware," and so on.

Here, however, is an example of what you can expect to see in the way of an actual job listing on OCC. This is what appeared when we selected one of the "writer" items on the menu produced by our keyword search:

```
[Jan 17] Writer (DE)
Page 1 of 1

Location: Delaware East Maine Northeast Oregon Northwest
Subject : Writer (DE)
From    : hwusa@occ.com

Caldwell Staffing Services
905 Shipley St.
Wilmington, Delaware 19801
Contact: Maryann Description:

We are looking for a skilled writer with experience in advertising and
promotions. Must also have excellent proofreading skills.

Status: Full Time
Salary: Competitive
Location: Wilmington
Job Category: 08 Computers & Technology
Closing date: Until Filled
Source: DENUCASTL

(C) 1994 Gonyea and Associates, Inc. Employers, to advertise your job
openings, call 813-372-1333. Job seekers, contact the employer or
recruiter listed in this ad, not Gonyea and Associates.
```

This certainly looks interesting. But, assuming this is a job you think you might like to apply for, what do you do next? As the information available via other OCC menus explains, job seekers should read each listing closely for instructions on how to respond. Some listings, for example, explicity state "No phone calls."

Others ask you to use an e-mail address. Note, however, that the line "From: hwusa@occ.com" appears in *all* listings. Look instead for a company-specific e-mail address, phone, or fax number. Failing that, use "snail mail," as online veterans call regular U.S. Post Office mail, to send your resume and cover letter to the employer.

Duplicate listings: More or less than meets the eye?

There may be less to the numbers of job listings presented by any online service than meets the eye, since careful study may reveal that the same job is listed multiple times under slightly different headings. There may be less still to the actual total number of unique jobs listed via electronic services, thanks to "borrowing."

For example, many of the jobs we looked at in OCC carried a plug for the "Talent Bank" and a copyright notice from Gonyea and Associates, Inc., the same company that operates the America Online Career Center. We found this curious, so we investigated.

We learned that nearly all the online job listing services "borrow" job listings from one another. Sometimes they work out an arrangement that lets them use another service's listing verbatim. Sometimes they simply rewrite a given listing to avoid copyright infringement. And sometimes they actually pick up listings from magazines and newspapers and add them to their databases.

On the other hand, why should we care? The point of an online job search is to use the power and reach of the computer to quickly zero in on the jobs that may be of interest. And to make your resume available to as many interested parties as possible.

From this perspective, duplication among online job databases is a good thing. By listing the same job under several different categories, they make it easier for job seekers to find. If you were a technical writer, for example, you might search on the keyword "technical" and

get one set of listings. Or you might search on the keyword "writer" and get a different set of listings. Under the circumstances, it's nice to know that you will find all the openings for technical writers in the database either way, even if it means that each job is listed once under "technical" and once again under "writer."

Resume searching

The main focus of this book is on finding employment, not on finding people to work for *you*. Still, it is important to note that the wonderful database-generated power of a computer can be applied to quickly finding people who are likely to have particular job qualifications. That's what the second item, "* Search Resumes" on the main OCC menu is all about.

Equally important, though, is that you, as a job seeker, can use this feature to bring up resumes of others in your field to see what *they* had to say about themselves. You can never, ever lie on a resume —not only is it unethical, you can easily be found out—but you can certainly learn from the efforts of others. So don't overlook the "* Search Resumes" feature, even if what you're really looking for is a job.

Search on the basis of whatever keyword you feel is most likely to appear in a resume of one of your global competitors. Once again, we recommend the plain-text approach offered by a system like Delphi when accessing this feature. But no one can contest the attractiveness of its World Wide Web page, as shown in Fig. 7-2.

Making the most of OCC

The Online Career Center is clearly one of the premier job-finding resources on the Internet. It shouldn't be your only stop on the electronic leg of your quest, but it should certainly be among your very first destinations. In our opinion, you will be best off if you log on and just let yourself run free, exploring items and trying features

Figure 7-2

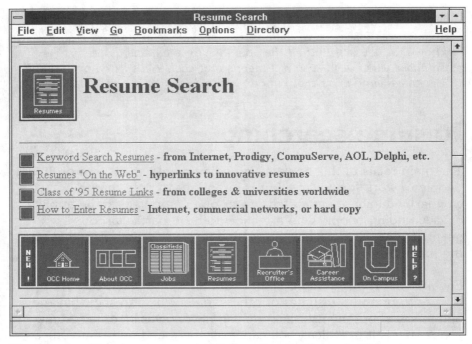

The Resume Search screen at the Online Career Center's Web site.

as your curiosity guides you. Don't worry about capturing anything to disk at this point.

Then, some time later, sign on using Delphi or some other text-based mode of access, open your capture buffer, and methodically begin working your way through each item on the main OCC menu. Naturally, some items will be of greater interest than others. But one you will not want to miss is the "Career Assistance" menu. When we were there, this listed nearly 50 job-search-related books, publications, and services. Each item on this menu led to a brief text file describing the item and telling you how to order or how to get more information.

⇨ Adding your own resume

Next, take the time to download and study several resumes. It really does not matter whether they are from people in your field or not. The key point is to put yourself in the position of an employer and judge these online resumes from that perspective. Which do you like, and why? Which do you hate, and why? Would *you* hire a given individual—would you even be interested in learning more about the person—based on the resume?

Use this hands-on field research to prepare your own resume. And try to make it as easy as possible for a potential employer to reach you. Be sure to include your voice phone (and fax number if you have one), as well as your land address, and the addresses of whatever electronic mailboxes you check every day. At the very least, you should include your Internet e-mail address, since anyone on any major online system can reach you there.

Then follow the OCC instructions (presented earlier in this chapter) for putting your resume on the system. But don't stop there. Give OCC a couple of days to add your contribution to its system; then check back to see how it looks. Remember, you can edit and resubmit your resume at any time.

The Online Career Center is a simply wonderful service. It's not perfect, of course. Nor is it comprehensive in its job listings. But then, no single service is either perfect or comprehensive. Thus, while you cannot limit your Internet and online campaign to OCC, you will find that it is an excellent place to start.

E-Span's Interactive Employment Network

AS many a seasoned online communicator knows, every online system or feature has its own "feel." That's because, like novels, movies, or any other work of art, an online feature is a creative endeavor that inevitably reflects the thoughts and mental approach of its creator.

The Interactive Employment Network created by E-Span is no exception. (We'll call it E-Span for short.) It started as a family operation and has a warm, family-style feel to it. At this writing, the company is over four years old and can boast a database that averages nearly 2,000 job listings at any given moment. The firm's mission is to provide "the highest quality jobs database and job search tools" available anywhere at no cost to the job seeker.

According to this Indianapolis-based company, its jobs database is posted on "14 online services, including Usenet newsgroups, the World Wide Web, CompuServe, America Online, Exec-PC, and GEnie." On the employer side, E-Span offers a variety of advertising packages starting at $35 a week, with quantity and frequency discounts available. Ads normally run for four weeks. For more information, call 800-682-2901.

How to post your resume on E-Span

Job seekers can browse the opportunities and—at no charge—submit their resumes to E-Span's resume bank via ASCII text-based disk, fax, mail, or e-mail:

E-Span, Inc.
8440 Woodfield Crossing Blvd., Suite 170
Indianapolis, IN 46240
Voice: 800-682-2901
Fax: 317-469-4508
E-mail: resume@espan3.espan.com

 # Points of access

It's impossible to know the order in which any reader will consume the chapters of a book. As writers, all we can do is present features and topics in the most appropriate order. Consequently, if you are reading this chapter before reading Chapter 6, then E-Span will be completely new to you. If you've already absorbed that chapter, however, then E-Span will be an old friend.

In any case, as one of the leading job- and employment-related features in the online world, E-Span is something you will not want to miss. So here are the main ways you can gain access:

➤ Use your favorite World Wide Web browser to access the URL specified as **http://www.espan.com/**.

➤ Look for their postings on the newsgroup **misc.jobs.offered** on the Internet.

➤ On CompuServe, key in go espan.

➤ On GEnie, key in espan.

➤ On America Online, follow the instructions in Chapter 6 to reach the Jobs area of AOL.

 # Your best bet

E-Span is a wonderful system, and we encourage you to access it by whatever means are available to you. However, since the company does not at this writing offer a Gopher, your best bet is probably to access it via America Online as discussed in Chapter 6. Or use your SLIP/PPP connection and Web browser to tap into the E-Span Web site. In our opinion the implementations of E-Span on CompuServe and GEnie are not up to snuff, at least not at this writing.

 # E-Span on the Web

To reach E-Span on the World Wide Web, load your favorite Web browser and tell it to use the URL **http://www.espan.com** to get to E-Span. A "welcome" screen of the sort shown in Fig. 8-1 will appear. From that point, you'll want to scroll and click and generally have a ball!

Figure 8-1

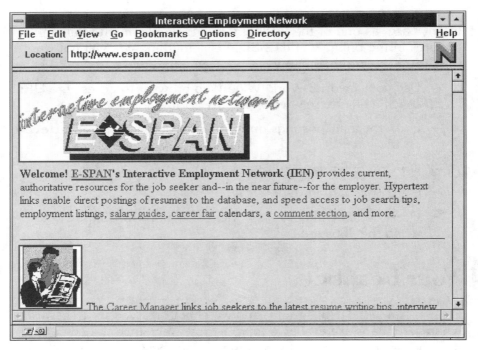

E-Span's home page on the World Wide Web.

E-Span has a lot of truly interesting features to offer—starting with its "Salary Guides." (See Fig. 8-2.) At this writing, you will find salary guides and reports for EDP (Electronic Data Processing) professionals, Engineering, and Accounting and Finance. We know of no other online jobs-oriented service that currently offers this kind of "juicy" information. Though, of course, such surveys are often published in relevant trade publications.

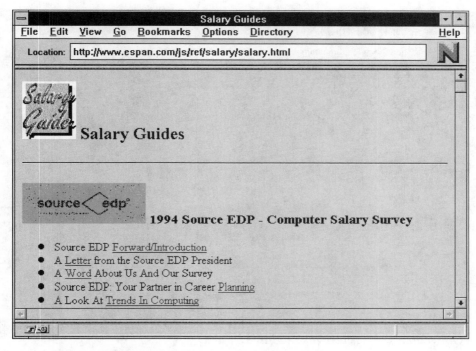

Figure 8-2

One of three detailed salary guides available on E-Span.

⇨ Job searching

The E-Span implementation on CompuServe forces you to use CompuServe's "Classified Ads" feature. As regular and active CompuServe users, we can tell you that this is a very weak feature. Much as we love CompuServe.

The E-Span Web implementation, however, is quite different. Figure 8-3 shows you the partial results of a search of the E-Span database for jobs for writers. And Fig. 8-4 shows you one of the resulting job listings. (There's a lot to be said for a steady paycheck compared to the vagaries of writing computer books for a living. That's why we keep using "writer" as a search term in our examples.)

Figure 8-3

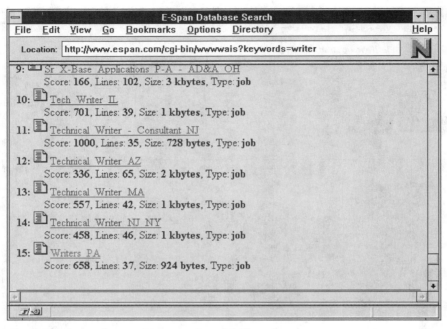

Our search for "writer" resulted in 15 "hits."

Figure 8-4

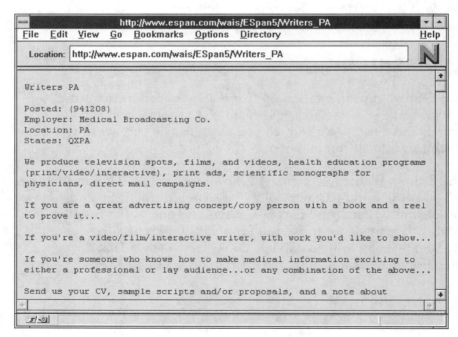

A sample job description from the E-Span database.

 # Many other features

As we have said, the best way to access E-Span on the Internet is via a World Wide Web connection. And, as you will see, there are lots of neat features at this Web site. These are E-Span features that may not be available any other way.

Certainly you will want to check out the E-Span "Reference Tools" as shown in Fig. 8-5. And you will want to look into the "Career Fairs by Region" feature illustrated in Fig. 8-6. You will find many other goodies in E-Span as well. Like the Online Career Center and the other features cited in previous chapters, E-Span is not the be-all and end-all—such a feature simply does not exist. But, as one of the leaders in online job postings and information, E-Span is definitely worth a thorough look.

Figure 8-5

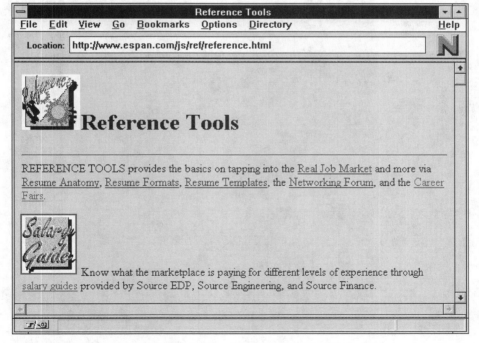

E-Span's Reference Tools menu on the World Wide Web.

Figure 8-6

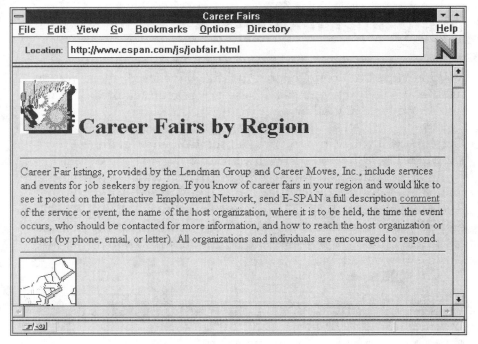

You can search for career fairs and special employment events on E-Span.

The *Occupational Outlook Handbook* online!

THE world doesn't suffer from any dearth of information about how and where to look for a job, how to prepare your resume, how to assess your skills, and so on. But no single source is quite like the *Occupational Outlook Handbook*. Comprehensive, well-organized, and frequently updated, it is truly a wonderful resource. Having used the print version often over the years in our writings about job searches and career guidance, we were thrilled to find that the *Occupational Outlook Handbook* is now available in electronic form via the Internet.

How to gain access

The *Occupational Outlook Handbook* is published each year by the U.S. Department of Labor's Bureau of Labor Statistics (BLS). The printed text and the electronic files are in the public domain and may be freely reproduced.

The University of Missouri, St. Louis, has taken the BLS at its word and made the book available electronically to everyone. To tap this resource, point your favorite Gopher at **umslvma.umsl.edu**.

That will take you to a menu that looks like this:

```
Univ of Missouri, St. Louis [umslvma.umsl.edu]
Page 1 of 1

1    About the UM-St.Louis Gopher                             Menu
2    Rights and Responsibilities of Computer Users at UM - St.Lou  Text
3    The Academic Divisions                                   Menu
4    Academic Bulletins and Course Schedules                  Menu
5    The Campus                                               Menu
6    The Community                                            Menu
7    The Computer Center                                      Menu
8    The Library                                              Menu
9    The Researcher                                           Menu
10   The Student Center                                       Menu
11   The World                                                Menu
12   Critical Information                                     Menu

Enter Item Number, SAVE, ?, or BACK:
```

The next step

Select Item 8, "The Library," from this menu and you will be taken to another menu, from which you should choose Item 10, "Government Information." That's where you'll find the *Occupational Outlook Handbook*.

```
The Library
Page 1 of 1

1    ===============UM-St. Louis Libraries gopher================    Text
2    ALL LIBRARIES INFORMATION      (Hrs., Announcements, Etc.)      Menu
3    - Thomas Jefferson Library Gopher  (Gopher)                     Menu
4    - Education Library Gopher         (Gopher)                     Menu
5    - Health Sciences Library Gopher   (Gopher)                     Menu
6    =========================================================       Text
7    Reference Desk            (Ask ?'s; Help Aids; Get Assistance)  Menu
8    Subject Area Resources    (e.g., Biology, Education, Business)  Menu
9    Library Catalogs          (UMSL LUMIN Online Catalog; Others)   Menu
10   Government Information     (US Federal & State Info & Docs)      Menu
11   Missouri Information       (Gophers, Documents, State Info.)     Menu
12   Periodical Indexes         (CARL, ERIC, SiteSearch, etc.)       Menu
13   Western Historical Man.    (Source Materials; Manuscripts)      Menu
14   Online Collection          (Full-Text Books, Journals)          Menu
15   Other Library Depts.       (Circulation, Interlibrary Loan, etc.) Menu
16   Search Library Gopher      (VERY Unstable!!!)                   Search


Enter Item Number, SAVE, ?, or BACK: 10


Government Information  (US Federal & State Info & Docs)
Page 1 of 1

1    +------NEW GOVT DOCS AT UM-ST. LOUIS AS OF 12/31/94--------+    Text
2    Lists of Latest US Government Documents of Interest Received   Menu
3    +----------------------------------------------------------+    Text
4    IN THE NEWS Govt. Documents (Current Interest & Full Text)     Menu
5    Depository Libraries by State (Text files from '94 Fedworld)   Menu
6    Government Documents Study Guides for UMSL      (Study Guide)   Menu
7    Government Info. Gophers, etc. on the Internet  (Gophers)      Menu
8    Library of Congress LOCIS                       (Catalog +)     Menu
9    Library of Congress MARVEL                      (Documents +)   Menu
10   State Government Gophers (by state)                             Menu
11   --------------FULL-TEXT GOVT. DOCUMENTS-----------------       Text
12   Army Area Handbooks                              (Overviews)   Menu
13   Background Notes-Dept. of State Country Information     NTD    Menu
14   Basic Guide to Exporting                                       Menu
15   Breaking Into the Trade Game: Small Business Guide to Export   Menu
16   Budget FY 1995, US Proposed [07 FEB 1994]                      Menu
17   Catalog of Federal Domestic Assistance (Search CFDA)          Search
18   CIA World Factbooks from 1992 - present                 NTD    Menu
```

```
19   Country Reports-Economic Policy & Trade Practices        NTD     Menu
20   Department of Commerce Economic Conversion (Post-military) I     Menu
21   Economic Reports of the President /1992-present                  Menu
22   Electronic Access to the White House          (How To Do        Text
23   Federal Register (searchable via Counterpoint Pub.)             Menu
24   General Agreement on Tariffs and Trade (GATT)                   Menu
25   Health Security Act (S. 2357 version 2, Mitchell, Aug. 8, 19    Menu
26   Health Security Act of 1993: Proposed Legis. by Title          Menu
27   Health Security Report 1993: Clinton Administration           Menu
28   International Business Practices Guide               NTD     Menu
29   International Narcotics Control Strategy Report 1993           Menu
30   Jail and Court Information Files (DOJ 1994)          NES     Menu
31   National Performance Review            (US Policy)            Menu
32 --National Information Infrastructure (NII)     (US Policy    Text
33 ---- Speech on NII by Al Gore, Jan. 11, 1994   (US Policy    Text
34   NAFTA-North American Free Trade Agreement      (Final Treaty  Menu
35   NAFTA-North American Free Trade Agreement Info. (Gopher)      Menu
36   Occupational Outlook Handbooks          (all editions 1992-   Menu
37   Overseas Business Reports                         NTD     Menu
38   Patterns of Global Terrorism 1994                 NTD     Menu
39   Small Business Administration Industry Profiles              Menu
40   Small Business Administration State Profiles                 Menu
41   U.S. Census Information                     (Statistic     Menu
42   U.S. Industrial Outlook - 1993 (NTDB Version)   (Statistic   Menu
43   U.S. Industrial Outlook - 1994 (NTDB Version)   (Statistic   Menu

Enter Item Number, SAVE, ?, or BACK: 36
```

This a long menu, to be sure. But we've presented the whole thing here because it's got so many goodies. Notice that you can use this last menu to access the Library of Congress (Items 8 and 9), log onto state Gophers (Item 10), get industry and state profiles from the Small Business Administration (Items 39 and 40), or read about the U.S. Industrial Outlook (Items 42 and 43).

To anyone interested in information, this is mind candy! None of these items contains actual job listings. But the background they provide can be invaluable. If nothing else, this kind of information can give you topics and facts you can use in your employment interview.

Plus, it can't hurt to be able to say to an interviewer, "Well, I was on the Internet the other day using the University of Missouri's Gopher at St. Louis. And I happened to notice in the U.S. Industrial Outlook section that widgets are on the decline. I wonder if I might ask what percentage of the XYZ Company's income depends on widgets?" Or words to that effect.

The *Occupational Outlook Handbooks* menu

You may very well want to Gopher back to this site sometime to explore further. But, tempting as it is to do so right now, we must stay focused on the issue at hand. So, let's select Item 36, "Occupational Outlook Handbooks," from the Government Information menu. Here's what you'll find there:

```
Occupational Outlook Handbooks          (all editions 1992- )
Page 1 of 1

1    *** Via the University of Missouri-St. Louis ***   Text
2    Occupational Outlook Handbook 1994-1995            Menu
3    Occupational Outlook Handbook 1992-1993            Menu

Enter Item Number, SAVE, ?, or BACK: 2


Occupational Outlook Handbook 1994-1995
Page 1 of 1

1    *** Via the University of Missouri-St. Louis ***        Text
2    Job Descriptions ONLY / 333 files alphabetically by title  Menu
3    ------------------------------------------------------------  Text
4    THINGS WORTH NOTING                                     Text
5    MESSAGE FROM THE SECRETARY                             Text
6    ACKNOWLEDGMENTS                                         Text
7    PHOTOGRAPH CREDITS                                     Text
8    CONTENTS                                                Text
9    KEYS TO UNDERSTANDING WHAT'S IN THE HANDBOOK          Text
10   SOURCES OF INFORMATION ON CAREER PREPARATION AND TRAINING  Text
11   ..Where To Learn About Job Openings                    Text
12   ..Keep the following in mind if you are using want ads:  Text
13   ..What Goes Into a Resume                               Text
14   ..Job Interview Tips                                    Text
15   TOMORROW'S JOBS                                         Text
16   EXECUTIVE, ADMINISTRATIVE, AND MANAGERIAL OCCUPATIONS  Menu
17   PROFESSIONAL SPECIALTY OCCUPATIONS                     Menu
18   TECHNICIANS AND RELATED SUPPORT OCCUPATIONS            Menu
19   MARKETING AND SALES OCCUPATIONS                        Menu
20   ADMINISTRATIVE SUPPORT OCCUPATIONS, INCLUDING CLERICAL  Menu
21   SERVICE OCCUPATIONS                                     Menu
22   AGRICULTURE, FORESTRY, FISHING AND RELATED OCCUPATIONS  Menu
23   MECHANICS, INSTALLERS, AND REPAIRERS                   Menu
24   CONSTRUCTION TRADES AND EXTRACTIVE OCCUPATIONS         Menu
25   PRODUCTION OCCUPATIONS                                 Menu
26   TRANSPORTATION AND MATERIAL MOVING OCCUPATIONS         Menu
27   SUMMARY DATA FOR OCCUPATIONS NOT STUDIED IN DETAIL     Menu
```

```
28   ASSUMPTIONS AND METHODS USED IN PREPARING EMPLOYMENT PROJECT    Text
29   SOURCES OF STATE AND LOCAL JOB OUTLOOK INFORMATION              Menu
30   DICTIONARY OF OCCUPATIONAL TITLES COVERAGE                      Text
31   REPRINTS                                                        Text
32   INDEX                                                           Text
33   RELATED PUBLICATIONS                                            Text

Enter Item Number, SAVE, ?, or BACK:
```

Space simply doesn't permit a discussion of all the items on this menu. But if you're in the job market or thinking about a career change, this is clearly an incredible resource.

Our advice is to open your comm program's capture buffer so that everything displayed on the screen will be recorded on disk. Then let your mind run free. Choose any and all of the menu items of interest and the resulting text will be saved on disk. Once you are offline, you can use your favorite word processor to clean up, edit, and read the file at your leisure.

Take the time to get to know what's available in the *Occupational Outlook Handbook*. It's definitely a resource you will want to tap again and again throughout your career.

10

Finding a job in government

A S we all know, state and federal government agencies buy everything from road salt to reconnaissance planes. And of course they have job openings for everyone from the most highly trained nuclear physicist to the least skilled day laborer. But how do you find out about government job openings?

That's what we're going to discuss in this chapter as we look at the Dartmouth Gopher's government jobs feature and the FedWorld BBS.

⇨ Way up north—to Dartmouth!

As we've said before, distance doesn't matter when you're on the Internet. And a good thing, too, since Hanover, New Hampshire is so far out of the way that it's the only Ivy League college your co-authors *didn't* visit as students. (As a band manager and a choir member, we got to travel, to see the East Coast, and, as it happens, to meet each other.)

Dartmouth has been a real leader when it comes to computing and computer geniuses. So it's really no surprise that the current crop of geniuses at Dartmouth College should offer a wonderful Gopher that just happens to include the mother lode of federal and state job information.

⇨ The Dartmouth College Gopher

To get started, point your Web browser to the URL location **gopher://DARTCMS1.DARTMOUTH.EDU:70/11/fedjobs**. (Remember that URLs are *case-sensitive!*)

Or Gopher to **dartcms1.dartmouth.edu**. (The eighth character in this address is the number "1," not the letter "l.") Choose "Job Openings in the Federal Government" and you will see a main menu that looks like this:

```
Page 1 of 1

1    Master list of All Network Mailing Lists    Menu
2    Job Openings in the Federal Government      Menu

Enter Item Number, SAVE, ?, or BACK: 2

Job Openings in the Federal Government
Page 1 of 1

1    Gopher and the Federal Job Openings Files      Text
2    About the Federal Job Openings Files           Text
3    Federal Gov't Position Announcements           Menu
4    Private Industry Position Announcements        Menu
5    Salary Pay Tables for Federal Civilian Emply   Menu
6    Specific Locality Pay Tables for Federal Emply Menu
7    Federal Job Classification                     Menu
8    Federal Group Occupational Requirements        Menu
9    Miscellaneous info useful to job applicants    Menu
10   Department of Defense Policies                 Menu
11   Disabled Persons and Veterans Policies         Menu

Enter Item Number, SAVE, ?, or BACK:
```

Where to begin

You will probably want to look at each of the items on the Dartmouth Gopher menu, but take our advice and *start* with Item 3, "Federal Gov't Position Announcements." The first two items on the main menu ("Gopher and the Federal Job Openings Files," and "About the Federal Job Openings Files") can be confusing. They will make a lot more sense later.

When you select Item 3 from the main menu, you will be taken to a second menu that gives you the opportunity to look at job openings for more than 50 government agencies and regional offices. The version shown here was edited to save space, but it preserves the flavor of what you will find:

```
Federal Gov't Position Announcements
Page 1 of 1

1    About the Federal Job FedJobs Openings Files    Text
2    Atlanta Openings                                Text
3    Atlanta Openings (cont'd)                       Text
4    Boston - Northern New England Openings          Text
```

```
5    Chicago Openings                              Text
6    Dallas Openings                               Text
7    Defense Financial Administration Services     Text
8    Defense Information System Agency Openings     Text
9    Defense Logistic Agency Openings              Text
10   Department of Commerce Openings               Text
11   Department of Interior Openings               Text
12   Department of Justice Openings                Text
13   Environmental Protection Agency Openings       Text
14   Military Bases in Europe Civilian Job Openings Text
15   Federal Miscellaneous Openings                Text
16   Washington Openings                           Text
17   Philadelphia Openings                         Text
18   Public Health Service Openings                Text
19   San Francisco Openings                        Text
20   San Juan, Puerto Rico Openings                Text
21   Senior Executive list Openings                Text
22   US Dept of Agriculture Openings               Text
     .
     .
     .
(etc.)

Enter Item Number, SAVE, ?, or BACK:
```

Each of the items on the "Federal Gov't Position Announcements" menu is a large text file containing dozens of brief descriptions of job openings. The information in the files is collected from the Office of Personnel Management (OPM) public bulletin board systems. The files are normally updated weekly. And the information is supplemented by job openings posted to BBSs run by other government agencies, postings to Internet newsgroups like **misc.jobs.misc** and **misc.jobs.offered**, as well as information forwarded to Dartmouth by colleges and state agencies around the country.

The files tend to be quite large, so make sure that you tell your communications software to capture incoming information to a disk file before you select an item. Once the file is on disk and you are offline, you can easily view it with your word processor. Better still, you can *search* it for key words like "summer job" or "architect" or some other topic of special interest.

Here are some examples to give you an idea of the format of the job listings and the type of information you'll find:

```
--------------------------------------------------------------------------
ANTHROPOLOGIST RESEARCH        GS-0190-07    01/17/95-01/31/95 PM0302
ANNOUNCEMENT #: PM0302                       DUTY LOCATION:
                                             NATICK, MA  1 JOB(S)

FOR APPLICATION INFORMATION CALL:
FED JOB INFO SPEC AT 617-565-5900
OR CONTACT: US OFFICE OF PERSONNEL MGMT
            BOSTON SERVICE CENTER
            BOSTON FEDERAL BLDG
            10 CAUSEWAY ST
            BOSTON  MA 02222-1031
            (617)565-5900

REMARKS: THIS POSITION PAYS $23,960 PER YEAR IS FULL TIME AND
         REQUIRES OVER-NIGHT TRAVEL OF 1 TO 5 NIGHTS PER MONTH.
         FORMS: MODIFIED RESUME, FORM C (1203-AW), AND SF-15
         (VETERANS PREFERENCE FORM, IF APPLICABLE)
--------------------------------------------------------------------------
CLERK                          GS-9999-02/03 12/27/94-01/31/95 PH5027
ANNOUNCEMENT #: 414-95                       DUTY LOCATION:
                                             ABERDEEN PR GR 5

FOR APPLICATION INFORMATION CALL:
JOB(S)QUINETTE HENDERSON AT 410-278-5795
OR CONTACT: U.S. ARMY
            ABERDEEN PROVING GROUND
            SUPPORT ACTIVITY
            ATTN: STEAP-CP-R
            ABERDEEN PG    MD 20115-5001
            (410)278-9175

REMARKS: THIS IS A SUMMER JOB.
--------------------------------------------------------------------------
COMPUTER ENGINEER              GS-0854-07/11 11/23/94-06/30/95 PM8338
ANNOUNCEMENT #: PM8338                       DUTY LOCATION:
                                             NEWPORT, RI   MANY JOB(S)
                                             NEW LONDON, CT  MANY JOB(S)

FOR APPLICATION INFORMATION CALL:
JEANNE LANGLOIS AT 401-841-3585
OR CONTACT: NAVAL UNDERSEA WARFARE CENTER
            1176 HOWELL STREET
            NEWPORT        RI 02841-1708
            (401)841-3317

REMARKS: POSITION REQUIRES APPROPRIATE EDUCATION AND OR
         SPECIALIZED EXPERIENCE IN RDT & E FOR SUBMARINE WEAPONS
         SYSTEMS.  NEW LONDON, CT APPLICANTS MUST BE WILLING TO
         RELOCATE TO NEWPORT RI IN APPROXIMATELY ONE YEAR. FORMS:
         SF-171 AND A COLLEGE TRANSCRIPT.
--------------------------------------------------------------------------
```

There are just two points to keep in mind. First, the city names in the "Federal Gov't Position Announcements" menu (Atlanta, Boston, Chicago, etc.) can be misleading. They refer to the location of the OPM office that posted the listing, not necessarily the location of the job opening. Second, before searching the file or files as we suggested, take the time to read through a few listings to get a sense of the abbreviations used. You will find, for example, that "MGMT" is frequently used instead of "management," so if you search for just the complete word, you'll miss many openings.

How to apply for a government job

As you review the text of various job openings, you will almost certainly be mystified by the forms that are required, the salary grade designations, and many other terms. But fear not. The Dartmouth College Gopher has it covered. Look again at the "Job Openings in the Federal Government" menu presented at the beginning of this chapter.

You will see headings for "Salary Pay Tables," "Federal Job Classification," and the like. But the item to select this time is Item 9, "Miscellaneous info useful to job applicants." This leads to information on all aspects of applying for a job with the federal government:

```
Miscellaneous info useful to job applicants
Page 1 of 1

1    Useful address CrossRef                              Text
2    OPM Regional Office Addresses                        Text
3    Requirements for working in CANADA                   Text
4    Getting Dialup Access to Internet Source Providers   Text
5    Rules for Direct Hire Authority                      Text
6    Early Out revised info for all Federal Civilians     Text
7    Federal Government Information System (FEDWORLD)      Text
8    Federal Retirement Information                       Text
9    Computer based application system                    Text
10   Gumprech Guide to Internet Government Info Sources   Text
11   Keller Guide to Internet Government Info Sources     Text
12   Requirements for working in JAPAN                    Text
13   JOBBANK: Computer Based Job Search                   Text
```

```
14   Federal Job Fairs                                  Text
15   How to get this info automatically from the server Text
16   Office of Management & Budget Computer Info Decree  Text
17   Access information for DIALUP job BB's              Text
18   Washington DC Personnel Office Address             Text
19   OPM RIF Manual for all Federal Civilians           Text
20   Frustrated postdoc BB info                         Text
21   Sources of the SF-171 Form in machine readable form Text
22   Selective Placement Office, Impaired Applic        Text
23   All State Employment Offices by state              Text

Enter Item Number, SAVE, ?, or BACK:
```

We will leave you to explore this treasure trove on your own. But first, one final tip for using the Dartmouth Gopher. When we last visited this site, the salary-related selections on the main menu were empty. Apparently the files were being updated. In any case, it provided the perfect opportunity to go in and get a file directly via FTP.

The files containing the salary tables have names like "95GS.TXT." They are plain text files that have been generated by printing a spreadsheet to disk. For instructions and a list of all the files on the Gopher, select Items 1 and 2 from the "Job Openings in the Federal Government" menu.

 # FedWorld!

In over a decade of searching for information online, we have always been enormously impressed by the databases prepared by the U.S. Department of Commerce. Thus we have never been surprised to find that each time we visit, FedWorld just gets better and better. It was created and is maintained by the National Technical Information Service (NTIS) division of the Department of Commerce.

FedWorld started out as a plain bulletin board system based on a typical personal computer. But it proved to be such a good idea that more incoming phone lines and computing power were added. Then in August 1994, FedWorld put up its own home page on the World Wide Web. (See Fig. 10-1.)

Figure 10-1

The FedWorld home page on the World Wide Web.

There are several ways you can connect with FedWorld by modem:

➤ BBS: 703-321-8020 (9600 bps, 8/N/1)

➤ FTP: ftp.fedworld.gov

➤ Telnet: fedworld.gov

➤ World Wide Web: http://www.fedworld.gov

The FedWorld Telnet site supports 50 simultaneous connections at this writing. But if all 50 connections are in use when you try to get in, don't leave. You'll be put on a waiting list for the next available connection.

⇨ Key points

The FedWorld system is largely self-explanatory. But it's important to remember that its mission is the dissemination of information of all sorts from the federal government. "Job openings" happens to be but one of many information categories. The Dartmouth Gopher, in contrast, really zeros in on government job openings and, indeed, offers virtually all of the same job openings information you will find on FedWorld.

Still, regardless of your means of access, you will find a menu item called "Federal Job Openings," which you should select. You will be taken to a submenu, similar to the one shown in Fig. 10-2, that includes items like the following:

➢ About the Job Announcements

➢ Atlanta Regional Federal jobs

➢ Chicago Regional Federal jobs

➢ Dallas Regional Federal jobs

➢ Philadelphia Regional Federal jobs

➢ San Francisco Regional Federal jobs

➢ Washington DC Regional Federal jobs

➢ National Federal jobs

➢ SES Federal positions available

➢ Public Health Service positions

➢ Federal jobs listed by state

➢ Atlantic overseas

➢ Pacific overseas

➢ Puerto Rico

➢ Virgin Islands

➢ Gateways with job info

➢ Federal Jobs E-mail Forum

➢ Jobs file library

Figure 10-2

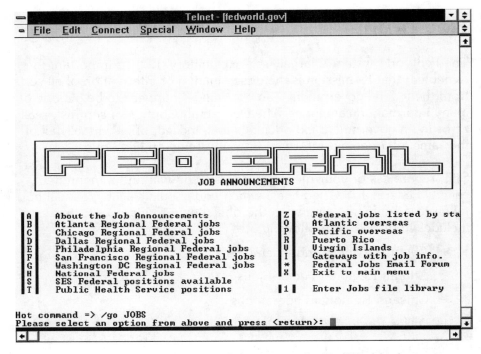

Here's what you can expect to see if you access the FedWorld job announcements via Telnet.

 # Conclusion

As we've said, job openings in the federal government are but one of the many areas covered by FedWorld, and the vast majority of those openings can be accessed using the Dartmouth Gopher. Nonetheless, FedWorld is such an impressive service that you should really give it a try as part of your online job search.

Here's where to get more general information about NTIS and FedWorld:

National Technical Information Service
5285 Port Royal Road
Springfield, VA 22161
Sales desk: 703-487-4650
Help desk: 703-487-4608

Finding a job in academe

CHAPTER 11

WHEN you recall that colleges and universities have been hooked into the Internet for over 20 years, it's not surprising that there is a huge amount of information about jobs in academe on the Net. The prime sources include:

➢ *The Chronicle of Higher Education*

➢ The Academic Position Network

➢ Academic Physician and Scientist

➢ The Texas A&M Web site

➢ The RiceInfo Gopher

➢ The University of Minnesota College of Education Bulletin Board

 # The Chronicle of Higher Education

The Chronicle of Higher Education is one of the leading publications in academe. Issued approximately every two weeks, this magazine typically carries 700 or more job listings for positions in faculty, research, and administration.

To tap into the online version, point your Gopher at **chronicle.merit.edu**. To access the World Wide Web version of this service, tell your Web browser to open the URL **http://chronicle.merit.edu/.ads/.links.html**.

Figure 11-1 shows you what you can expect when going in via the Web. Here, however, we will focus on the Gopher version of this service.

 ## The Gopher version

When you Gopher to **chronicle.merit.edu**, you will see a menu like the one shown here. If you are at all interested in the academic world, you will find this Gopher menu particularly enticing and will

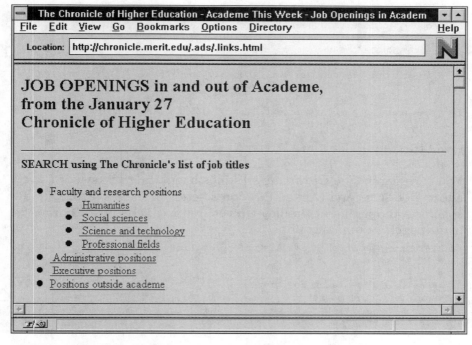

Figure 11-1

The Chronicle of Higher Education *on the Web.*

want to explore it further. However, for now, we've selected Item 16, "Jobs in and out of Academe: More than 630 openings."

```
Page 1 of 1

1    New in "Academe this Week"                              Text
2    A Guide to The Chronicle of Higher Education, Jan. 27, 1995   Menu
3    Organizations in Academe                                Menu
4    —News of Organizations                                  Text
5    —Information provided by the Annenberg/CPB Project       Menu
6    Information Technology in Academe                        Menu
7    —News of Information Technology                          Text
8    —Information provided by Lotus Development Corporation   Menu
9    Finances and Personal Planning in Academe               Menu
10   —News of Finances and Personal Planning                 Text
11   —Information provided by Fidelity Investments            Menu
12   —Information provided by TIAA-CREF                       Menu
13   Best-Selling Books in Academe: a new list               Text
14   Events and Deadlines in Academe                         Menu
15   Facts and Figures on U.S. higher education              Menu
16   Jobs in and out of Academe: More than 630 openings      Menu
```

```
17   Information about The Chronicle's publications        Text
18   About "Academe this Week": search tips and more      Menu

Enter Item Number, SAVE, ?, or BACK: 16

JOBS in and out of Academe: more than 630 openings
Page 1 of 1

1    SEARCH using The Chronicle's list of job titles   Menu
2    SEARCH using any word or words of your choosing    Menu

Enter Item Number, SAVE, ?, or BACK: 1
```

You can search *The Chronicle's* listings by job title or keyword. We chose "job title" and worked through a series of menus leading to a specific job opening at Bradley University for a Director of Forensics and Speech Communication:

```
SEARCH using The Chronicle's list of job titles
Page 1 of 1

1    Faculty and research positions    Menu
2    Administrative positions          Menu
3    Executive positions               Menu
4    Positions outside Academe         Menu

Enter Item Number, SAVE, ?, or BACK: 1

Faculty and research positions
Page 1 of 1

1    Humanities               Menu
2    Social sciences          Menu
3    Science and technology   Menu
4    Professional fields      Menu

Enter Item Number, SAVE, ?, or BACK: 1

Humanities
Page 1 of 1

1    Art and art history             Menu
2    Classics                        Menu
3    Communication                   Menu
4    English as a second language    Menu
5    English language and literature Menu
6    Foreign languages and literatures Menu
7    History                         Menu
8    Literature                      Menu
9    Music                           Menu
10   Philosophy                      Menu
11   Religion                        Menu
```

```
12   Theater                              Menu
13   ACADEME THIS WEEK's main menu        Menu

Enter Item Number, SAVE, ?, or BACK: 3

Communication
Page 1 of 1

1    Communication—Dana College—NE                              Text
2    Faculty Positions—Otterbein College—OH                     Text
3    Faculty positions—SUNY-Oneonta—NY                          Text
4    Faculty positions—Wagner College—NY                        Text
5    Forensics - Speech Communication—Bradley University—IL      Text
6    Joyce Dissertation Fellowship—Gustavus Adolphus College     Text
7    Scls-Performing Arts, Art-Design, Commnctn—Northern Arizo   Text
8    Speech Communication—Centenary College of Louisiana—LA      Text

Enter Item Number, SAVE, ?, or BACK: 5

Forensics - Speech Communication—Bradley University—IL
Page 1 of 1

Position: Forensics - Speech Communication
Institution: Bradley University
Location: Illinois

Forensics/Speech Communication: Director of Forensics/Speech
Communication. Tenure-track Assistant professor to direct Bradley
University's national championship speech team and teach courses in basic
speech, small group, interpersonal, and persuasion. Teaching in other
areas of interest also possible. Applicants must have experience in
teaching and coaching forensics teams. Department members are expected to
conduct and publish research, advise students and perform professional
and university service. Applicants must have an earned doctorate. ABDs
with early, definite completion dates will be considered . . .(etc.)
```

 # Making the most of it

What you see here is exactly what we saw when we tapped into this
feature. The system is set up to guide you to what you want via a
series of ever more specific menus. Subject areas covered included
Art and Art History, Classics, Communication, English Literature,
Music, Philosophy, Religion, and Theater. But that's just when we
were there. Naturally, subject areas and listings change as open
positions are filled and as new jobs become available.

Academic Position Network

The Academic Position Network (APN) is an online service accessible worldwide through Internet. It provides notice of academic position announcements, including faculty, staff and administrative positions. Included are notices of announcements for post-doctoral positions and graduate fellowships and assistantships.

APN's goal is to provide academic institutions with a faster, more accurate, and a more cost-effective way of reaching candidates. Through the use of international communications networks, position announcements receive a broader exposure to potential candidates.

Academic position announcements are transmitted to APN staff by e-mail or fax and placed on the network within 24 hours. Institutions pay a fixed one-time fee to post an announcement. There is no size limit on APN announcements, and they are kept online in the database until the posting organization asks to have them removed or the closing date has been reached. There is no charge to browse and search APN files.

To access APN, point your Gopher at **wcni.cis.umn.edu 11111**. Or, if you want to use a Web browser, specify the URL **gopher:// wcni.cis.umn.edu 11111**/. Figure 11-2 shows what you can expect when you tap into the Gopher using a graphical Web browser like Mosaic or Netscape Navigator.

When you access the APN feature using a text-based Gopher of the sort you will find on Delphi, however, here is what you can expect to see:

```
Academic Position Network [wcni.cis.umn.edu]
Page 1 of 1

1    Search for Files                 Search
2    William C. Norris Institute      Text
3    Placing an Announcement          Text
4    About the APN                    Text
5    World Conference 1995            Menu
6    A P N Information & Instructions Text
7    Alabama                          Menu
8    Alaska                           Menu
```

```
 9   Arizona                        Menu
10   Arkansas                       Menu
11   Australia                      Menu
12   California                     Menu
13   Canada-British Columbia        Menu
 .
 .
 .
64   Wisconsin                      Menu
65   Wyoming                        Menu

Enter Item Number, SAVE, ?, or BACK:
```

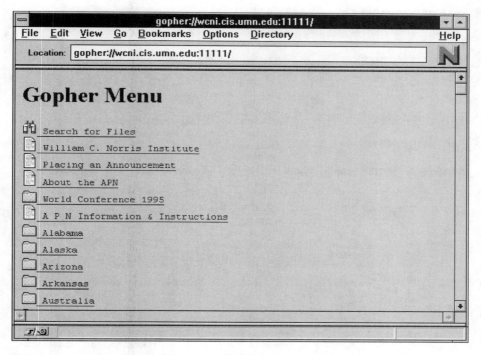

Figure 11-2

The Academic Position Network's Gopher seen via a Web browser.

If you were to pick the very first item, "Search for files," you would be prompted for a keyword. When we responded with "admissions," the system gave us the menu shown below from which we chose Item 4:

```
Search for Files
Page 1 of 1

1   Pennsylvania/Pennsylvania College of Technology/Director of   Text
```

```
2    Pennsylvania/Pennsylvania College of Technology/Dean of Stud    Text
3    Ohio/Miami University/Executive Director - Hamilton Campus       Text
4    Minnesota/St. Mary's College of Minnesota/Residence Life Dir    Text
5    California/California State University-Long Beach/Tenure-tra     Text
6    Tennessee/University of Tennessee, Knoxville/Associate Direc     Text
7    Tennessee/University of Tennessee, Knoxville/Research Coordi     Text
8    Oklahoma/Northeastern State University/Registrar                Text
```

Enter Item Number, SAVE, ?, or BACK: 4

Minnesota/St. Mary's College of Minnesota/Residence Life Director
Page 1 of 1

Date of APN entry: 11-9-94

COUNTRY/STATE: MINNESOTA

UNIVERSITY/COLLEGE: St. Mary's College of Minnesota
                          Winona Campus

POSITION TITLE: Residence Life Director

REVIEW SCHEDULE: Applications will be accepted immediately.
                          Anticipated starting date is January 1995
                          or earlier.

SUBMITTAL INSTRUCTIONS: Send a letter and resume with three current
                          references to:

CONTACT PERSON/OFFICE: Office of Residence Life
                          St. Mary's College of Minnesota
                          700 Terrace Heights
                          Campus Box 9
                          Winona, MN 55987-1399

        Phone: 507/457-1406 for further information.

DUTIES AND RESPONSIBILITIES:

Under the direction of the Dean of Students and the Vice
President for Student Development, the Director of Residence Life
is responsible for the management of all aspects of the
residential life program at Saint Mary's College. The Director,
in-residence on campus, is accountable for the over-all
administration of the residence life program; selection, training
and supervision of hall directors/graduate assistants . . . (etc.)

Qualifications: Master's degree and three years of experience
in college or university residence life; knowledge of developmental
stages of college students . . . (etc.)

Clearly, if you are interested in a job at a college, university, or similar institution, you cannot afford to ignore APN. It's not comprehensive, but then what job listing service is? Leave no stone unturned! Tap in to APN and plan to spend an hour or more exploring.

 # Academic Physician and Scientist

Academic Physician and Scientist (APS) is a centralized resource for positions in academic medicine. It claims to be the largest, most comprehensive collection of positions in academic medicine. The publication itself is produced bi-monthly, and it includes news from the world of medical education. It's mailed free-of-charge to every faculty physician, scientist, senior resident, and fellow at 126 medical schools and their affiliated teaching hospitals.

To subscribe or advertise a position, contact:

Academic Physician and Scientist
Voice: 916-939-4242
Fax: 916-939-4249
E-mail: info@acad-phy-sci.com

To gain access, point your Gopher at **aps.acad-phy-sci.com**. As soon as you log on, you will see a menu like this:

```
Page 1 of 1

1    About Academic Physician and Scientist          Text
2    Contacts at Academic Physician and Scientist     Text
3    Administrative Positions                         Menu
4    Basic Science Positions                          Menu
5    Clinical Science Positions                       Menu
6    Food and Drug Administration (FDA) Opportunities Menu
7    NIH Opportunities                                Menu
8    Gopher Jewels                                    Menu

Enter Item Number, SAVE, ?, or BACK:
```

You will want to explore each menu item on your own. But to give you a flavor or what you'll find, we chose "Clinical Science Positions" and found jobs listed in each of the following categories:

Anesthesiology
Biomedical Ethics
Clinical Pharmacology
Community and Preventive
  Medicine
Dermatology
Emergency Medicine
Epidemiology
Family Medicine
Genetics
Neurology
Nuclear Medicine

Obstetrics and Gynecology
Occupational and
  Environmental Medicine
Ophthalmology
Orthopedic Surgery
Pathology
Pediatrics
Physical Medicine
Psychiatry
Radiology
Radiation Oncology
Surgery

For an example of what the APS Gopher looks like when you log in using Netscape Navigator or some other graphical browser, see Fig. 11-3.

The Texas A&M Web site

What we have shown you so far is more than the beginning but far less than the end of job-related features for the academic community. There are at least three other locations you should try, if you are interested in a job in academe.

Start with the Texas A&M Web site (shown in Fig. 11-4) at the URL address **http://ageninfo.tamu.edu/jobs.html#otherorgs**. You will find a menu listing dozens of colleges and universities. Click on those you're interested in to read about available positions.

The RiceInfo Gopher

You will also want to tap into the RiceInfo Gopher. As you may recall, we introduced you to this wonderful resource in Chapter 5. Gopher

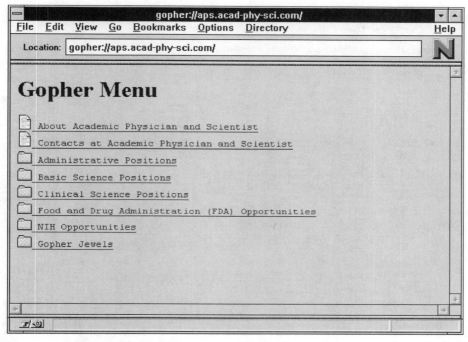

Figure 11-3

The main menu for the Academic Physician and Scientist Gopher, displayed with a Web browser.

to **riceinfo.rice.edu** and look at the main menu as before. Choose "Information by Subject Area"—it was Item 9 when we were there—and then "Jobs and Employment" (Item 28).

With a Web browser, you can specify the URL **gopher://riceinfo .rice.edu:70/11/Subject/Jobs**.

This leads to a menu that had nearly 75 headings when we looked at it. Here's a greatly shortened version to give you an idea of what you will find:

```
Jobs and Employment
Page 1 of 1

1   About this directory                                      Text
2   Academe This Week/Chronicle of Higher Education           Menu
3   Academic Physician and Scientist (APS): jobs in academic med   Menu
4   Academic Position Network (from cis.umn.edu)              Menu
5   Biomedical Engineering (from the Whitaker Center, Purdue)  Menu
```

Figure 11-4

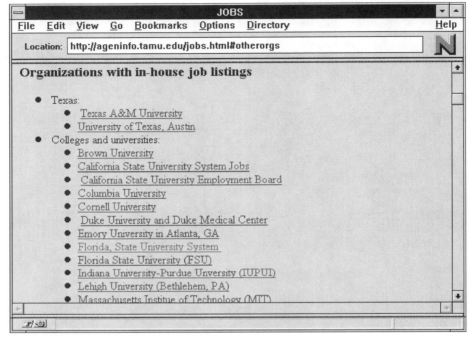

The Texas A&M World Wide Web location.

```
6    College & Research Libraries job postings by job title       Menu
7    Florida state university system                              Menu
8    History (from U. Kansas H-Net)                               Menu
9    Indiana University-Purdue University at Indianapolis (IUPUI)  Menu
10   Job Openings for Economists                                  Menu
11   Lehigh University (Bethlehem, PA)                            Menu
12   MedSearch America (healthcare/biotech job search services)   Menu
13   Memorial University of Newfoundland                          Menu
14   North Carolina Office of State Personnel                     Menu
15   Occupational Outlook Handbook (all editions 1992- )          Menu
16   Online Career Center (msen.com)                              Menu
17   Oregon State University (in "OSU This Week...")              Menu
18   Pennsylvania State University                                Menu
19   Princeton University                                         Menu
20   U.S. government jobs listings (from dartmouth.edu)           Menu
21   USENET newsgroup bionet.jobs                                 Menu
22   USENET newsgroup biz.jobs.offered                            Menu
23   University of California at Berkeley                          Menu
24   University of California at Santa Cruz (academic)            Menu
25   University of Delaware (salaried and hourly)                 Menu
26   University of Utah                                           Menu
27   University of Wisconsin                                      Menu
28   Washington State University                                  Menu
```

```
29  Yale University                                        Menu
 .
 .
 .
(etc.)

Enter Item Number, SAVE, ?, or BACK:
```

As you can see, the RiceInfo Gopher gives you yet another way to access some of the other features discussed in this chapter. But it also can take you right into various colleges and universities to check their job postings.

Wanted: Teachers for K through 12!

Finally, if you are looking for a position as a teacher at the kindergarten, elementary, or high school level, check out the Gopher-based bulletin board operated by the University of Minnesota's College of Education. Point your Gopher at **rodent.cis.umn.edu 11119**. Or load your Web browser and open the URL **gopher:// rodent.cis.umn.edu:11119/**.

This Gopher includes hundreds of brief job postings for positions in administration, media specialty, psychology, and counseling; early childhood development and elementary education; secondary education, vo-tech, and phys-ed; and higher education as well. It is thus quite easy to browse this system by specialty.

Or you can run a search the way we did. The process is shown in Figs. 11-5, 11-6, and 11-7. We started with the main Gopher menu shown in Fig. 11-5 and clicked on the Search function. As you can see in Fig. 11-6, we opted to search on the word "art." Figure 11-7 shows you the beginning of a list of matching job openings.

Figure 11-5

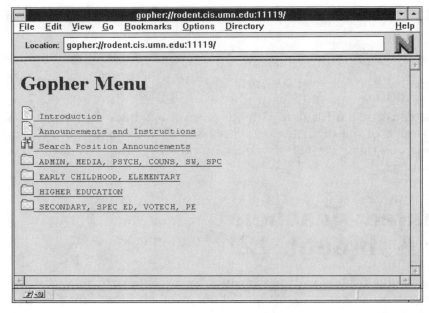

The Gopher greeting screen at the University of Minnesota's College of Education.

Figure 11-6

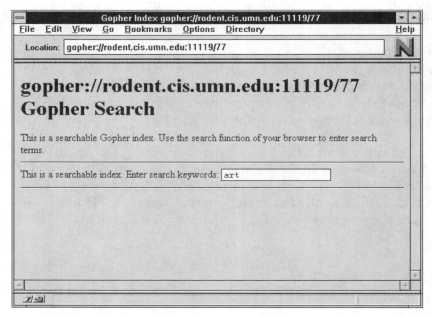

Searching for "art" on the University of Minnesota Gopher.

Figure 11-7

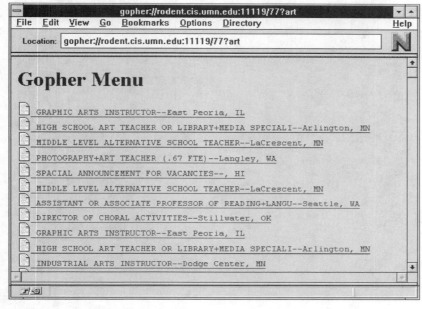

And here are the job openings we found . . .

Here's what the first one, an opening for a Graphic Arts Instructor in East Peoria, Illinois, looked like:

```
GRAPHIC ARTS INSTRUCTOR—East Peoria, IL

Page 1 of 1

GRAPHIC ARTS INSTRUCTOR
  SEND APPLICATION TO:
    Doris Symonds
    Illinois Central College
    One College Dr
    East Peoria, IL 61635
  PHONE:  309-694-5113
  FAX:
  NUMBER OF POSITIONS:  1
  SALARY:
  START DATE:
  VACANCY POSTING DATE:  December 8, 1994
  APPLICATION DEADLINE:  Mar 24, 1995
  POSITION DESCRIPTION AND/OR QUALIFICATIONS:
    Need bachelor's in industrial technology with specialty in
    graphic arts. Send letter of appl., resume, and transcripts.
```

12

Finding a job in science & high tech

CHAPTER 12

IMAGINE that you're an employer. Imagine that you want to find someone who speaks French. Where would you post such a job listing? There are lots of possibilities, of course, but surely one obvious spot would be in a French-language newspaper or magazine.

The same logic applies to jobs in scientific fields and jobs with high-technology companies. Computer programmers, mathematicians, scientists, and so on, are among the most active users of the Internet. So what better place for a company to post job openings, and what better place for such people to look.

In this chapter we will plug you into the two leading Internet-based features for people interested in science- and high-tech-related jobs: CareerMosaic and The Monster Board.

CareerMosaic

Probably the very first place anyone interested in jobs in science and high technology should look is CareerMosaic. To get there, open the URL **http://www.careermosaic.com**/. You'll see a screen like the one shown in Fig. 12-1. If this screen has a more professional feel than many of the Web pages you may have encountered, there's a good reason.

CareerMosaic was created by Bernard Hodes Advertising, Inc. In our opinion, it offers one of the best examples of how a World Wide Web feature *should* be done. The screens are full without being "busy." The graphics are sharp, but they do not take a long time to appear. In short, whether you're interested in a high-tech job or not, you may want to visit this site just to see how it's done.

CareerMosaic currently offers job information for more than two dozen high-tech firms in the San Francisco Bay area. Employers pay for the privilege of having a snazzy Web page on CareerMosaic, where they can recruit potential employees by presenting company profiles and information about benefits, work sites, and special benefits, all with the click of an icon. (See Fig. 12-2.)

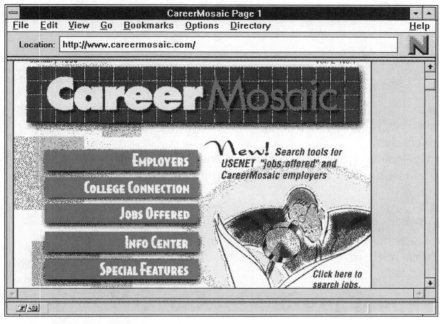

CareerMosaic's opening screen.

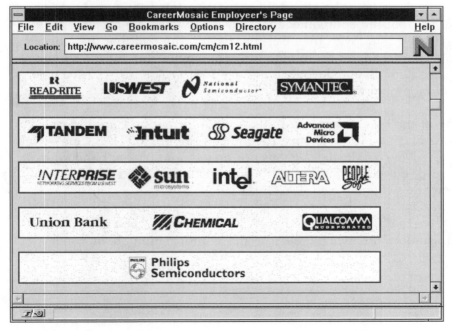

Here are just some of the firms with a presence on CareerMosaic.

Figure 12-1

Figure 12-2

Companies offering information on CareerMosaic at this writing include:

AMD	PeopleSoft
Adaptec	Philips Semiconductor
Altera	Qualcomm
Biogen	Read-Rite
Cedars-Sinai Medical Center	Schlumberger
Chemical Bank	Seagate
First USA Bank	Sequent Computer Systems
General Instrument Corporation	Sprint International
Intel	Sun Microsystems
Intuit	Sybase
Miller Brewing	Symantec
National Semiconductor	Tandem Computers
Northern Telecom	US WEST

 # Company profiles on CareerMosaic

CareerMosaic, unlike many other services, usually offers quite a lot of information about the companies that post job openings. Certainly the fact that the companies themselves are paying a monthly fee has something to do with this. But there's also the fact that the kinds of employees many of these high-tech companies find most desirable tend to be in demand—hence the need to "sell" a prospective new hire on joining the firm.

One of the best examples of this is the information CareerMosaic offers on Sun Microsystems. As you can see in Fig. 12-3, Sun's Web page on CareerMosaic displays not only the employee handbook and ID card, but also a red Ferrari. And a picture of Scott McNealy, the company's founder and C.E.O.

But where do you go from here? Turns out that if you click on the workstation, you will be taken to more information about Sun

Figure 12-3

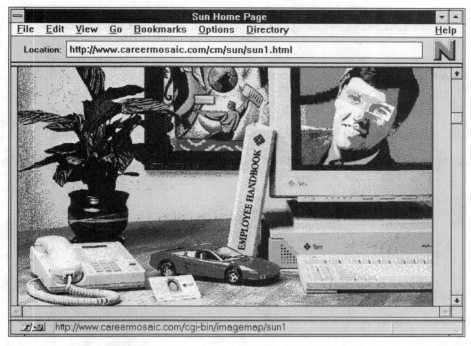

The Sun Microsystems home page on CareerMosaic. But why the Ferrari? (See the text to find out!)

products. Clicking on the ID badge takes you to "career opportunities" with the company. The employee handbook leads to information on company benefits, and the phone gives you the firm's phone number. Is that cool, or what?

But what about the red Ferrari? Well, when you click on that, you will be taken to a feature that discusses the corporate culture of Sun Microsystems. The Ferrari belongs to Sun's Bill Joy, and it symbolizes the April Fool's Day tradition at Sun. Apparently, on that day in 1987, Mr. Joy discovered his Ferrari in a . . . But why give it away? Go to the site and see if you don't just ache to work at Sun Microsystems after you read about their corporate culture. (Which, of course, is the point.)

Searching for jobs on CareerMosaic

You can, of course, search CareerMosaic for a particular job rather
than focusing on a single company. You'll find an example of that in
Figs. 12-4 through 12-6. We searched for programmer positions and
zeroed in on one particular listing with a firm in Milpitas, CA.

Figure 12-4

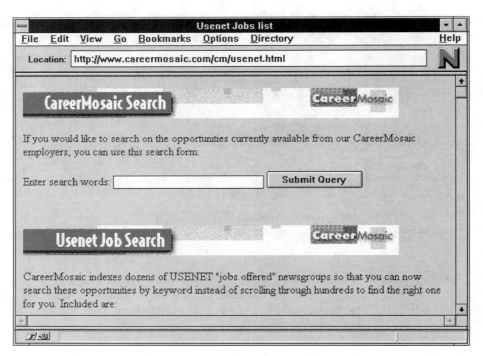

Of course, you can search for jobs on CareerMosaic . . .

Figure 12-5

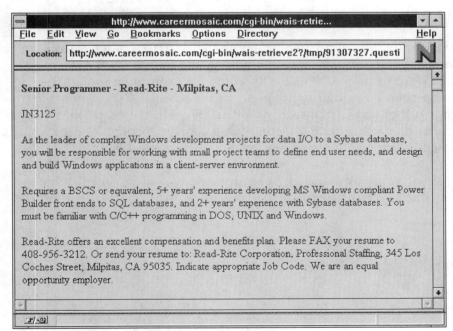

Search of CareerMosaic Jobs Database

File Edit View Go Bookmarks Options Directory   Help

Location: http://www.careermosaic.com/cgi-bin/cm_jobs

Score: 1000, Lines: 13, Bytes: 807
Senior Programmer - Chemical Bank - New York, NY

Score: 1000, Lines: 14, Bytes: 791
Senior Programmer - Read-Rite - Milpitas, CA

Score: 1000, Lines: 10, Bytes: 976
Systems Software Programmer - Read-Rite - Milpitas, CA

Score: 1000, Lines: 10, Bytes: 1006
Systems Software Programmer - Read-Rite - Milpitas, CA

Score: 1000, Lines: 10, Bytes: 1184
Systems Analyst/Programmer Analyst - Seagate - Scotts Valley, CA

Score: 1000, Lines: 9, Bytes: 495

When we searched CareerMosaic for "programmer," lots of listings appeared.

Figure 12-6

http://www.careermosaic.com/cgi-bin/wais-retrie...

File Edit View Go Bookmarks Options Directory   Help

Location: http://www.careermosaic.com/cgi-bin/wais-retrieve2?/tmp/91307327.questi

Senior Programmer - Read-Rite - Milpitas, CA

JN3125

As the leader of complex Windows development projects for data I/O to a Sybase database, you will be responsible for working with small project teams to define end user needs, and design and build Windows applications in a client-server environment.

Requires a BSCS or equivalent, 5+ years' experience developing MS Windows compliant Power Builder front ends to SQL databases, and 2+ years' experience with Sybase databases. You must be familiar with C/C++ programming in DOS, UNIX and Windows.

Read-Rite offers an excellent compensation and benefits plan. Please FAX your resume to 408-956-3212. Or send your resume to: Read-Rite Corporation, Professional Staffing, 345 Los Coches Street, Milpitas, CA 95035. Indicate appropriate Job Code. We are an equal opportunity employer.

Here's a sample CareerMosaic listing for a programmer position.

 # The Monster Board

The Monster Board is the East Coast's answer to CareerMosaic. More than likely, as time goes on, CareerMosaic will become less West-Coast oriented and the Monster Board less East Coast. But right now, the distinction is pretty clear.

The Monster Board was created by the advertising firm, ADION Information Services, Inc. And at this writing, over 90 percent of the jobs it lists are from several dozen companies in the northeast. Companies offering job listings include: ADION, Bradlees, Braintree Hospital Rehabilitation Network, Brooktrout Technology, Computer Express, Dragon Systems, Electronic Book Technologies, Fidelity Investments, General Cinema Theaters, Johns Hopkins University-Applied Physics Lab, Open Environment Corporation, PCs Compleat, Unitronix, and Wellfleet.

You can browse, search, and select information on the basis of company name, location, discipline, and specific job title. Once you've selected jobs you're interested in, you can enter your own resume in an online form. Most jobs are in computing-related fields, but marketing, communications, and other positions are included as well.

To get to the Monster Board, open the URL **http://www.monster .com**. If you're operating with anything less than a 28.8 modem, you'll want to take ADION's advice and turn off the graphics. (As you'll notice from their home page shown in Fig. 12-7, they make ample use of large "monster" graphics!) For Mosaic users, that means clicking on Options and selecting "Delay image loading." For Netscape, click on Options and turn off "Auto Load Images."

Once you're at the Monster Board home page, scroll down to the icons (Fig. 12-8) and explore.

Figure 12-7

Welcome to the Monster Board!

Figure 12-8

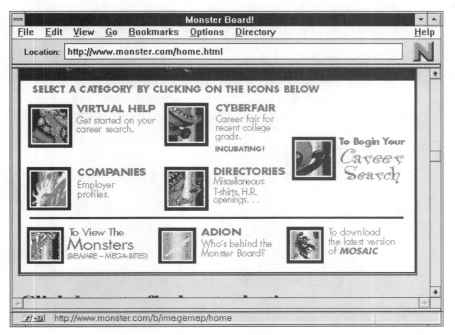

Click on an icon to search the Monster Board for career assistance, company profiles, career fairs, monsters, whatever . . .

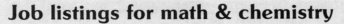

Job listings for math & chemistry

It seems entirely likely that as the Internet continues to expand and develop, more discipline-specific job-listing services will emerge. In fact, this is already happening. If you are trained in chemistry or in mathematics, you won't want to miss the two services described here.

- *Academic Chemistry Employment Clearinghouse*

  One of the few resources in its field, this site is just getting started. When we were there, it had only about a dozen positions. But as word spreads, that is bound to improve. Subfields covered include analytical chemistry, biochemistry, inorganic, organic, and physical chemistry. This "clearinghouse" is offered by Northern Illinois University's Chemical Informatics Program.

  *To get there, point your Gopher at **hackberry.chem.niu.edu** and select "Academic Chemistry Employment Clearinghouse" from the menu that will appear. Or open the URL **gopher://hackberry.chem.niu.edu:70/11/ChemJob**.*

- *American Mathematical Society*

  The American Mathematical Society maintains a large (200+) list of job openings for men and women with advanced degrees in mathematics. Most positions are for jobs in academe, including separate listings for postdoctoral fellowships, but there are opportunities in both private business and nonprofit organizations as well. The list is updated almost daily.

  *To get there, point your Gopher at **e-math.ams.com**. Select "Professional Information for Mathematicians" and then "Professional Opportunities for Mathematicians" from the resulting menus. Or open the URL **gopher://e-math.ams.com**.*

13

Finding a job in health care

CHAPTER 13

ANYONE listening to the current debate on health care reform and paying attention to (or experiencing!) the aging of the "Baby Boom" population can't help but conclude that health care is likely to be a growth area for many years to come.

If this is the field you're involved in or considering, then you absolutely must tap into MedSearch America. To gain access via the World Wide Web, open the URL **http://www.medsearch.com** and visit the MedSearch America home page (Fig. 13-1). Or point your friendly Gopher to **gopher.medsearch.com** and choose "Msen Career Center" and then "MedSearch America" from the menus that will appear. You'll see menus that look like this:

```
MedSearch America
Page 1 of 1

1    What's New on MedSearch America (TM)          Text
2    All About MedSearch America (MSA)             Menu
3    How To Post your Resume Online                Menu
4    MedSearch America Membership                  Menu
5    --> Featured Employers                        Menu
6    --> Search Jobs                               Menu
7    --> Search Resumes                            Menu
8    Recruitment Services Network - New!           Menu
9    Health Career Resources                       Menu
10   Health Career Articles                        Menu
11   Healthcare Industry Outlook                   Menu
12   Frequently Asked Questions                    Menu
13   Limitation and Disclaimer of Liability        Text
14   Copyright (C) 1994 MedSearch America, Inc.    Text
15   Employers/Members Only [password required]    Telnet

Enter Item Number, SAVE, ?, or BACK: 2


All About MedSearch America (MSA)
Page 1 of 1

1    Introducing MedSearch America                        Text
2    What Types of Employer is MedSearch America For?     Text
3    How to Become an Employer/Member                     Text
4    Employer Membership Benefits                         Text
5    What Type of Job Seeker is MedSearch America For?    Text
6    How to Post Your Resume Online                       Text
7    How To Update/Delete Your Online Resume              Text
8    Healthcare Job Seeker Benefits                       Text
9    Job Seekers Without Internet Access                  Text
10   How to Contact MedSearch America                     Text
11   Copyright (C) 1994 MedSearch America, Inc.           Text
12   MedSearch America (TM)                               Text

Enter Item Number, SAVE, ?, or BACK:
```

Figure 13-1

Here's the MedSearch America Web home page.

Introducing MedSearch America

MedSearch America bills itself as the first and only Internet employment advertising and communications network designed specifically for the health care industry. They offer detailed employer profiles, job listings, resume postings, industry and career resources, electronic communications, online career discussion groups, online exchanges between employers and job seekers, and direct links with related government resources on the Internet.

The service can be accessed around the clock, seven days a week, using either Gopher or a World Wide Web browser. (See the nearby sidebar for more details on the specific services MedSearch offers job seekers and employers.)

MedSearch: Features for job seekers & employers

Here are the services MedSearch offers to individuals seeking employment in health care industries, followed by the services offered to member companies/employers.

Services for job seekers:

- *Online resume posting by e-mail (or direct upload on the Web).*
- *Access to job listings searchable by geographic location, job category, job title, keyword, employer name, and primary industry.*
- *Detailed company profiles.*
- *A recruitment services network.*
- *Health career articles written by career experts.*
- *Health career resources that include a job search guide (tips, books, periodicals, software packages, articles), detailed descriptions of occupational titles, relocation guide, listings of career events, and associations.*
- *Health care industry information.*
- *Paper resume posting (first page free).*
- *A health care career newsgroup.*

Services for employers:

- *Direct dial-up account to independently access and use all MedSearch America member services.*
- *Worldwide company advertising on Gopher.*
- *Worldwide company advertising on a company Web home page, complete with photos, graphics, and sound.*
- *Worldwide and unlimited job advertising (public and blind ads).*
- *Searchable resumes by keyword, occupation, desired work status, resume title, and job search location.*
- *Unlimited hiring from job-seeker users at no extra charge.*
- *Online prescreening of job candidates.*
- *In-house outplacement capabilities.*
- *Personal e-mail address.*
- *Direct access to government agencies on the Internet.*

What types of job seekers use MedSearch?

MedSearch job seekers include medical and nonmedical professionals who want to work in a health care-related environment, as well as students interested in pursuing a health care career.

To take advantage of their services, MedSearch America recommends that you have one or more of the following qualifications:

➤ Work experience in a health care or related setting.

➤ Skills that are transferable to a health care setting, such as business/management, law, computer, etc.

➤ A degree in health care, or a field such as business, science, engineering, or insurance.

➤ Specialized health care education, training, and/or certifications.

MedSearch America charges *no placement fees* to you or to subscribing employers for any position—permanent, temporary, internship, contract, traveling, or volunteer—at any level.

 # What types of employers use MedSearch?

MedSearch America member companies include a wide range of health care and related organizations looking for qualified professionals at all levels, and in all fields of expertise. Here are some examples of the types of companies you'll find:

Biotechnology Firms	Federal and State Agencies
Blood Banks	Geriatric Clinics
Cancer Treatment Centers	Health Insurance Companies
Dental Offices	HMOs
Drug Retail Companies	Hospital

Laboratories	Pharmaceutical Companies
Long-Term Care Facilities	Primary Care Facilities
Medical/Surgical Instruments	Public Health Departments
Companies	Rehabilitation Centers
Mental Health Centers	Sports Medicine Clinics

 # MedSearch via the Web

As we have said many times, in general, you will be better off accessing almost any site using good old Gopher. That's still true here, but you owe it to yourself to check out the MedSearch America Web site. The company has prepared pages that look great but do not take too long to appear. In short, they have used graphic images intelligently. See Figs. 13-2 and 13-3 for examples of what you can expect at the Web site.

Figure 13-2

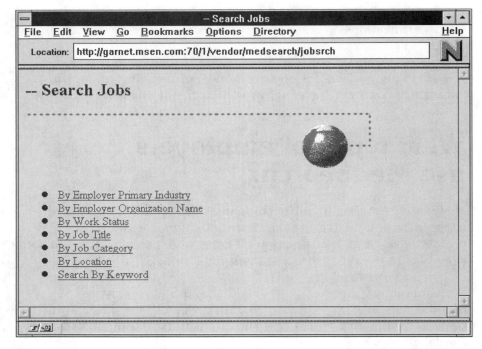

This page appears when you click on "Search Jobs" from the MedSearch America home page.

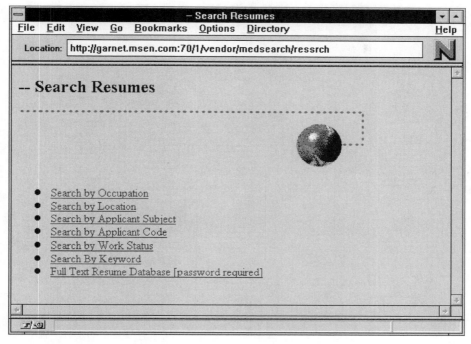

Figure 13-3

And this page appears when you click on "Search Resumes" from the MedSearch America home page.

⇨ Conclusion

Health care is going to be a major issue for the foreseeable future. But the jobs, salary levels, work load, and everything else about every aspect of the professions involved is likely to change. The entire health care industry is in flux.

Which is why it is a very good idea for anyone contemplating a health care career to check with MedSearch America first. Use this service to get a sense of what skills are in greatest demand, what such jobs pay, and what your future is likely to be if you pursue a particular health care-related job or profession.

Finding a job
in business

ALL right. We admit it. The term "business" here is a bit loose. Our thought is that this is everything *but* jobs in government, academe, science/high tech, and health care. A broad area—a *very* broad area. Nonetheless, when you see what we've got to show you here, you'll agree that this is a chapter you won't want to miss. Regardless of your current specialty or career plans.

The Yahoo List at Stanford

The key site is the Yahoo List at Stanford University. This is a "list of lists" presented in World Wide Web format. That means you can click on any resource or other item on the list and be taken to the site where it is located immediately, thanks to hypertext links.

To get to the Yahoo List, open the URL **http://akebono.stanford .edu/yahoo**/. This will take you to the feature's main screen. As you will then see, Yahoo has lists of lots of different things—Art, Business, Computers, the Economy, Education, Entertainment, Environment and Nature, Events, Government, Health, Humanities, Law, News, Politics, Reference, Regional Information, Science, Social Science, and Society and Culture.

If you click on "Business" and then on "Employment," you'll see a screen like the one shown in Fig. 14-1. You can go directly to this screen, of course—bypassing the Yahoo greeting screen—by specifying the URL **http://akebono.stanford.edu/yahoo/ Business/Employment**/. (Don't forget that URLs are case-sensitive, so be sure to key this one in exactly as shown here.)

Go for "Companies"

As you peruse this list, you'll see some familiar names: CareerMosaic, the Academic Position Network, RiceInfo, and so on. Needless to say, you can reach all of those sites from here. But we're interested in business jobs, so we suggest you click on "Companies." That will take you to a submenu. (All of the boldface items with numbers in parentheses on the Yahoo List lead to submenus.)

Figure 14-1

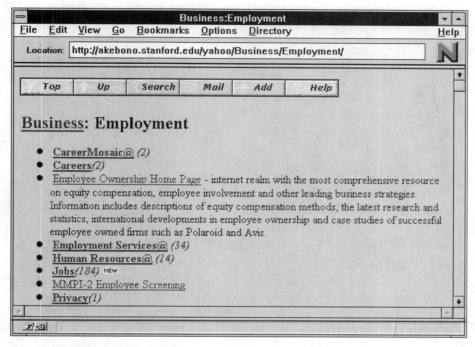

The Yahoo List's Business/Employment screen.

When we were there, the submenu listed nearly 70 companies. In general, we found that all the firms offer company profiles, background, and recruiting information. But many include specific job listings as well. Click on the company name and you'll be transported to its home page. (See Figs. 14-2 and 14-3 for examples.) Here are just some of the companies you'll find:

Advanced Micro Devices	Intuit, Inc. (Quicken)
Amdahl Corporation	Microsoft
Andersen Consulting	PeopleSoft
Bank of America	Qualcomm, Inc.
Chemical Bank	Read-Rite
Cisco	Seagate
College Pro Painters	Sun Microsystems
Compaq Computer Corporation	Symantec
Electronic Data Systems (EDS)	Tandem Computers, Inc.
Fidelity Investments	TRW
Forrester Research, Inc.	Union Bank
Intel	US West

Figure 14-2

A people-oriented recruiting poster from Andersen Consulting.

Figure 14-3

Chemical Bank's snazzy home page.

Samples: Fidelity, College Pro, & Union Bank

As we said, each company offers profile and recruitment information, but not all include listings for specific job openings. The only way to know for sure is to actually click on the company's name and see where you are taken. Companies and specific offerings will undoubtedly change over time, but at this writing, the features offered by Fidelity Investments, College Pro, and Union Bank are representative.

Fidelity Investments

When you click on Fidelity, you will be taken to a screen like the one shown in Fig. 14-4. Note that the division listing career opportunities is Fidelity's Investment Technology Team, so you can assume that most of the offerings will involve computing skills.

Figure 14-4

Career opportunities with Fidelity Investments.

When we were there, over 25 positions were described, including:

> ➤ Director, Equity Workstation Products
>
> ➤ Director of Operations
>
> ➤ Manager—UNIX Systems Administration
>
> ➤ Data Modelers/Database Architects
>
> ➤ Investment Data Specialist
>
> ➤ EIS Application Specialist
>
> ➤ C++ Developers: GUI, Database (Multiple Opportunities)
>
> ➤ Software Quality Assurance Analyst

Here is a job description of the sort you will find using Fidelity's feature:

```
Business/Systems Analysts (Multiple Opportunities)

Create new investment systems using knowledge of the
investment process and systems analysis and design,
focusing on GUI design, data modeling, object modeling,
and applications requirements definition. Exceptional
organizational, communication, and writing skills
required. Major new projects include building the next
generation of Equity Portfolio Management Systems, Global
Equity Trading Systems, Risk Management Systems, Fixed
Income/Foreign Exchange Trading Systems, and High Income
Research Systems. You will be working directly with our
Fund Managers, Securities Analysts and Traders.

JOB CODE:        03C
```

At the end of the Fidelity page there is some information that briefly sketches the benefits the company offers, plus an e-mail, fax, and land address to which you are asked to forward your response.

 # College Pro Painters

Painting houses has long been an attractive summer job for college students and K-12 teachers. Some years ago, however, a company called College Pro Painters was formed to bring order and professional management to this activity. As a result, regardless of

where you live, you can hardly avoid seeing the distinctive yellow College Pro signs in front of houses being painted these days.

When you remember that students at most colleges and universities these days have easy, free access to the Internet, you can see why it makes such good sense for College Pro to use the Net to recruit. Whoever put up the company's home page on the Web could use a quick remedial course in spelling. But we're willing to overlook that in light of a truly cool feature: forms!

Not all World Wide Web browser programs currently support online, interactive, real-time forms. But if yours does, you can try it out on College Pro. Figure 14-5 shows you the College Pro greeting page. But notice that there's a button to "Apply On-line!" built right into the page. Click on that and you will be taken to a page called "Application for Manager Position."

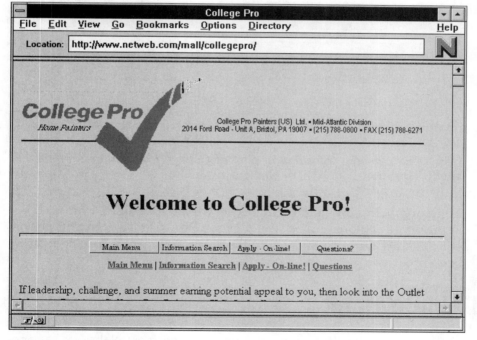

Figure 14-5

Welcome to College Pro Painters!

This will tell you the locations, phone numbers, and e-mail addresses of the company's regional offices. And it will lead you to the actual application. Figure 14-6, for example, shows you the screen that is used to fill in your name and address information. Simply move your cursor to the appropriate blank and type in the information.

Figure 14-6

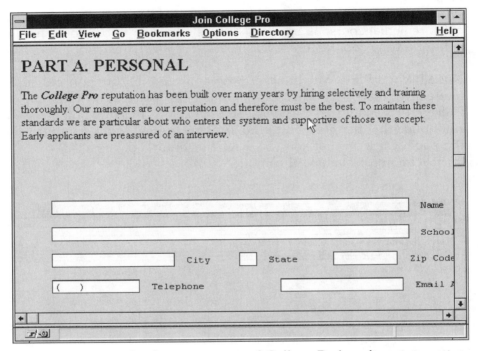

Here's the personal information part of College Pro's online, interactive, application form.

In theory, your completed application will be forwarded to the appropriate regional office. But College Pro suggests that you phone your nearest office to make sure that your application has indeed been received.

 # Union Bank

California's Union Bank presents perhaps the most elaborate feature of all. As you can glean from Fig. 14-7, you can learn about its

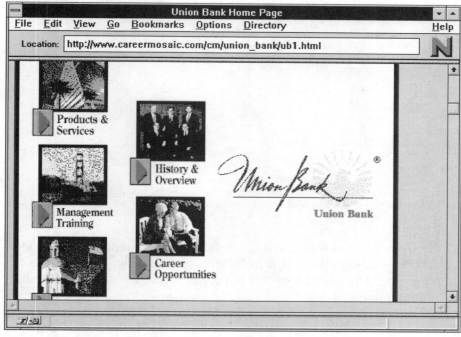

Figure 14-7

Here's Union Bank's greeting screen. Just click and go!

products and services and company locations, and you can get a brief history and overview of the organization. Most important, of course, is the "Career Opportunities" section.

Unlike the Fidelity Technology Team or College Pro, Union Bank is using the Web to recruit people for its 15-month Management Training Program, graduates of which can expect to be assigned to a wide variety of positions. That is undoubtedly why the bank offers such a broad array of information.

The jobs one can look to after graduating from the bank's management training program include Credit Officers, Financial Service Officers, and Business Relationship Officers. You will find descriptions of each of these positions online. The Union Bank feature ends, of course, with "How to Apply." But interestingly—and, we think, significantly—prospective applicants are first given the following advice:

If you plan on interviewing for these positions, it is
important that you prepare yourself with some library
research. Union Bank history, financial strategies, etc., can
be located in both CD ROM disk and ON-LINE Services. When
searching these services, be sure to search on Union Bank of
California. Recommended programs are:

```
CD ROM
ON-LINE-SERVICE
MOODYS
NEXUS
WALL STREET JOURNAL
FIRST SEARCH
ABI INFORM
DISCLOSURE Laser D-annual reports of the bank
INFOTRAC-Investext reports prepared by investment bankers
BUSINESS DATELINE-reports on California business
```

Aside from the fact that there is no database or online system called
"NEXUS"—though there is a wonderful system called *Nexis*—this is
good advice. Chapter 18 of this book will introduce you to a number
of online databases.

For a more complete description, see *The Information Broker's
Handbook—Second Edition* by Sue Rugge and Alfred Glossbrenner,
published by McGraw-Hill. Whether or not you want to become an
information broker yourself, this book can be invaluable in showing
you how to look things up online.

Conclusion

There is simply no doubt about it. At this writing, the vast majority of
jobs offered via the Internet are in government, academe, and high-
tech professions. Given the roots of the Internet, this is perfectly
understandable.

Fortunately, however, business offerings are catching up. The
Stanford Yahoo List is simply *the* place to start if you're interested in
jobs in general business. Our advice is to check it regularly, especially
the sections we've told you about here. And bear in mind that we've
profiled only three of some 70 companies. More firms are sure to

come online and those who are already there are sure to expand their job listings and offerings.

It'll take a little time. But before too long, offerings for jobs in business are sure to catch up with the high-tech, academic, and government entries.

Part 3

Job search tools and techniques

15

Preparing your resume & putting it online

CHAPTER 15

THE chapters in Part 2 showed you where to find listings of job openings online. In this part of the book, we'll look at what to do next and at the electronic techniques you can use to uncover the hidden job market, starting with some suggestions on preparing your resume.

⇨ The *real* purpose of a resume

As anyone who has ever looked for a job knows, your resume is your primary *sales* document. What most new job seekers don't know, however, is exactly what their resumes are selling. Many assume that by summarizing their background, education, and experience—and putting the best possible spin on everything—their resumes are intended to sell an employer on *hiring* them.

Wrong!

The real purpose of a resume is to get you a personal *interview*. By neatly summarizing your background and experience, your resume does indeed convey a sense of your qualifications. A company looking for an assistant marine biologist isn't likely to consider someone whose resume lists no scientific training whatsoever. But they might consider someone with a degree in a related area and a history of summer jobs in the field.

It all depends. And, naturally, there is never any way to know, at least not with entry-level positions for college graduates or middle-level positions for those who already have an employment history. For example, at one end of the spectrum, the ability to type a certain number of words per minute, or state certification in some trade, may be an absolute requirement. And at the highest levels, a proven track record running a multimillion-dollar sales organization may be an absolute.

Flexibility in the middle

But in between, where the vast majority of the jobs are, things are often more flexible and fluid. If a specific skill is required—like proficiency with some computer language—there's no point in wasting a personnel manager's time if you don't have it. But put yourself into the shoes of the personnel officers and human resource managers of the world.

In the first place, you would never hire anyone without a personal interview. And you'd be suspicious of someone who would accept a job, sight unseen, as it were. So there you are with positions to fill. Who among the scores of people who have sent you resumes are you going to interview? You know from experience that you'll have to interview several people for each position, and you know that some will be clearly suitable, some clearly unsuitable, and some who don't fall into either category.

The candidates you select on the basis of this initial interview will probably be asked back to interview with their prospective bosses and co-workers. Meetings will be held; there will be discussions of the various candidates; and ultimately a job offer will be made.

 # Who would *you* interview?

References may or may not be checked, though any more it is so easy to check public records via computer that many employers routinely run a pre-employment check. (The second edition of *The Information Broker's Handbook* by Sue Rugge and Alfred Glossbrenner devotes an entire chapter to public records searching, especially as it relates to pulling up pre-employment information.)

So again, the question is, if you're a personnel officer, which applicants are you most likely to want to interview. Assume that everyone meets the minimum requirements for education, skills, or whatever. You can't interview everyone. So on what basis would you choose one resume over another?

We've got some ideas on the subject that have to do with being interesting, even intriguing. But, more importantly, by the time you've learned to use the resources discussed in this chapter, you'll have some pretty clear ideas of your own.

We've never heard anyone mention this, but one of the unique and incredibly significant features about job-hunting online is that you get to look at lots and lots of resumes submitted by *other* people. You get to play "Personnel Officer for a Day" and consider which of these resumes you like and which you do not. You get to ask yourself, "Would I want to interview this person?" Short of actually serving in a personnel office, there's no other easy way to do that.

 # Resume preparation advice

This is not a book about resume writing, however. There are lots of books devoted to that subject alone. One of the best, in our opinion, is *The Electronic Resume Revolution* by Joyce Lain Kennedy and Thomas J. Morrow (John Wiley & Sons). Ms. Kennedy is the career columnist for the Los Angeles Times Syndicate, and her book includes many excellent examples of the various styles of resumes now in use. You will also want to see the companion volume *The Electronic Job Search Revolution* by the same authors.

Ms. Kennedy's thesis in a nutshell is this: Employers have begun to use scanners and optical character recognition (OCR) software to sort and select paper resumes. And they're using other software to do the same with resumes they find online. Since the software involved has been programmed to search for certain keywords, you had better make sure that those keywords can be found in your resume.

Ms. Kennedy even suggests that some types of resumes should start with a heading called "Keywords," followed by your occupational objective, work experience, and so on. It's a new concept, which is very much the point of her book, but it's hard to see how it could hurt, regardless of how widespread the practice of scanning resumes really is.

For hands-on advice from Ms. Kennedy herself, visit the Online Career Center and select "Career Assistance." You will find two items on the resulting menu—they were 12 and 13 when we were there—that give you tips from her books. The other items on that menu are worth a look as well, but we were disappointed to find that most of them merely tell you about books or other resources. Ms. Kennedy's items, however, offer solid advice.

You can reach the Online Career Center by Gophering to **occ.com**. Or use your Web browser to specify the URL **http://www.occ .com/occ/**. See Chapter 7 of this book for more details.

 # Paper resume tips

You don't need any advice from us on form and content. The books about resume writing devote entire chapters to these topics. In our opinion, though, whether paper or electronic, resumes should be visually inviting. Nothing is more off-putting than huge blocks of single-spaced text. Even if such a document contains the desirable keywords to make an initial computer-based first-cut, the human being who has to look at it will take one glance and pass over it.

If you're unsure of your judgement in this, you can always hire a resume-writing service to help you. The September 1994 issue of *Online Access* had several good tips as well:

> ➤ Don't be afraid to phone human resources departments to ask if they scan resumes.

> ➤ Don't use fancy typefaces or graphics.

> ➤ Do send your resume on high-quality white paper.

> ➤ Don't fold your resume, since the creases may ruin the scan.

> ➤ Make sure your resume includes your electronic mail address, as well as your land address, voice phone, and fax number if you have one.

 # Online resume tips

The requirements for a super-looking online resume are different. So different that you will need to prepare both a paper resume and an electronic version. As mentioned, you will definitely want to spend some time collecting and considering the resumes uploaded by others.

But when it comes time to prepare your own, the key concept to keep in mind is "lowest common denominator." This is crucial because you have no idea what kind of computer or software the person who downloads your resume may be using. Hence, the following tips.

 # Only plain ASCII text

Regardless of the word processing software you use, make sure that you save your electronic resume to disk as a plain, pure, non-document mode, 7-bit ASCII text file. We've used this string of adjectives because of the different ways word processing programs refer to plain text.

In line with this, you should use *paired asterisks* to symbolize italics (*like so*). This convention has developed through long tradition. It's necessary because there is no underlining, boldface, or real italics in plain text mode. Similarly, a lowercase letter *o* is often used for a "bullet."

Dealing with downloaded resumes

Unfortunately, while you may be wise enough to use the "lowest common denominator" of plain ASCII text, many others may not. And that includes many of the newest online users. One can hardly blame them, after all. The resume or other text they prepare in WordPerfect or Microsoft Word looks great on their screens. Because they have never taken the time to understand the tools they are using, it never occurs to them that their beautiful text will look like garbage on someone else's screen.

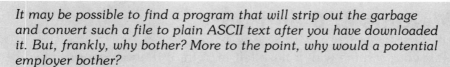

It may be possible to find a program that will strip out the garbage and convert such a file to plain ASCII text after you have downloaded it. But, frankly, why bother? More to the point, why would a potential employer bother?

If someone is such a novice, such a "newbie," that they don't know the importance of using plain ASCII text for e-mail and other telecommunications messages, what could they possibly have to say that would be of value?

This is a brutal assessment, we know. But it is necessary, if only to deliver a wake-up call. Three or four years ago, people would cut you a break. They would even take the time to message you back that you should resend using plain text. But not now.

The fact is that these days there are tens of thousands of people just like you who do know how to use this technology and have taken the time and expended the effort to learn how it all works.

In our opinion, you should do likewise. And if you need some help in this regard, you might look for some of our other books. (For information, send a blank e-mail message to **info@books.com**, our auto-responder. Within a few minutes, you'll find a message from us in your Internet mailbox.)

Meanwhile, here's how to steal a march on your competitors. Virtually all of the resumes you download from an FTP site—or capture via Gopher or some other text-based means of access—will indeed be plain text. But the files you capture as World Wide Web files (using Netscape Navigator, NetCruiser, or some other Web browser program) will be in HTML format. That stands for Hypertext Markup Language, and it means that they will be riddled with HTML codes.

The HTML codes are plain ASCII text, but they do mess things up. That's why you need to know about a little program called DE-HTML.EXE for Windows/DOS users. We mentioned this program in Chapter 4, and noted that it's available from Glossbrenner's Choice on the disk called Internet 8, World Wide Web Essentials. But you can find this utility on the Internet as well.

This program will strip out the HTML codes and produce a plain ASCII text file from the resume file—or any other Web/hypertext file your Web browser program has saved to disk. You can load any ".HTM" file into your Web browser and scroll through it as if you were online. But you may find the plain text files produced by DE-HTML.EXE to be easier to read and use.

 # Margins at 0 and 65

Start your resume with a flush left margin of 0 and indent as need be to set off bulleted paragraphs, but keep your right margin at 65.

There are two reasons for this. First, if you indent your entire resume, you end up with several columns of blank spaces. To a computer, a blank space character (ASCII 32) is the same as a text character that you can see. Adding 10 blank spaces before each word (by indenting your entire resume), may look good on the screen. But what if the employer's word processing software is set to tell the printer to indent 10 spaces? Your resume will be printed out with a 20-character indent, which could result in the truncation of some of your lines.

Second, the human eye has difficulty reading 80-character lines, but 65-character lines are perfect.

 # Start with a block of keywords

Attaching a list of keywords to a database "record" has long been standard practice in the online world. Indeed, the main job of an *indexer/abstracter* is to read magazine articles, prepare brief summaries or abstracts, and decide which keywords should be attached to the articles in an electronic database.

Those keywords may or may not appear in the abstract or in the article itself. For example, an article about the history of gunpowder might not actually include the word *munitions*. But the indexer/abstracter might add that word to the keyword list on the assumption that anyone searching for information on munitions would be interested in an article about gunpowder.

In our opinion, it is thus perfectly appropriate to attach a list of keywords to your electronic resume. Some online services make it possible for someone to search on the basis of a resume's contents, in which case your list of words may generate a "hit" for the searcher. But even if a given service has not yet implemented keyword searching, including a list of such words still doesn't hurt. At the very least, it gives the person who looks at your resume a quick snapshot of you. And certainly it demonstrates that you are really plugged into the requirements of the Information Superhighway.

 # Test before uploading—and after

It's true that preparing and testing the technical details of an electronic resume can be a time-consuming process. But once you've done it, you will be able to quickly blast your resume to all kinds of electronic locations.

Whether you're a DOS, Windows, or Macintosh user, after you have saved your resume to disk as a plain text file, bring that file back in again to make sure that it contains nothing but text. If you are a DOS 5 or DOS 6 user, you may want to check your pure text file resume with the EDIT program that comes with DOS. (EDIT produces clean text files.) Or, at the DOS prompt, enter the command TYPE filename.ext ¦ MORE, where *filename.ext* is the actual name of your file. That will display the file one screen at a time in DOS, and any non-text characters it may contain will be revealed.

Finally, once you've uploaded your resume, go back in and download it. Be aware that there will probably be a delay of some sort between the time you transmit your resume and the time it becomes available for searching and downloading. But do not neglect to check your own resume after uploading it to any system. Make sure it looks the way you want it to look.

 # Develop a *system*

Everybody's different. Perhaps you can remember that your resume on System A is due to expire next week, while the copy you transmitted to System B is good for the next six months. Or maybe, with so many things going on, you are likely to forget that you transmitted and tested your resume on System B a month ago. Whatever.

Clearly it makes sense to map out a game plan. The information provided in this book is designed to alert you to the possibilities and to give you some indication of what to expect from each feature or service. But only *you* can decide where you want to post your resume, and only you can keep track of what you have done, when it is time to repost your resume, and so on.

 # Making a little list

The best way to take greatest advantage of the job-finding resources available via the Internet and other online systems is to start by just letting yourself go. Don't worry about remembering this or that, or this system's strong points and that one's weak points. Get your feet wet. Get your entire body wet. Take a quick look at everything, and give yourself time to digest it all.

Then go back to each system and, notepad at your side, begin to explore it in depth. Ask yourself: Does this system have the kind of jobs I'm looking for? Would my ideal employer be likely to search this system for me? How long does a given resume stay on this system? And so on. On the basis of your notes, decide where you want to post your resume. (And, once again, take the time to download your resume from a system to make sure everything went through all right.)

Next, consult your notes about the specific job listings or company profiles you have found. Who gets a resume? And how should you transmit or mail it? When you decide these questions and take action, make sure you make a note to follow up. That means telephoning or sending e-mail to the appropriate individual or address at the employer's location: Did you receive my resume? Is the position still open? Do you have any questions or points that need to be clarified?

 # Making your presence felt

In short, make your presence felt. At least for those jobs you find really, really desirable. By definition, mediocrity is the norm. So, in

some cases, all you have to do is show a little spark, a sincere interest, some real enthusiasm, to stand out from the pack.

It doesn't always help. But it never hurts! After all, given two equally qualified candidates, who would you yourself rather hire—the person who merely submits a resume or the person who submits a resume and then follows up a week later to express a genuine interest in the job or other opportunities with the company?

Someone once said that 90 percent of success in life is just showing up. Someone else once said, "The secret to succeeding at this company is to show up . . . on time . . . dressed to play!" In the case of this particular company, that meant a conservative suit, with a long-sleeved cotton shirt, unobtrusive tie, knee-high stockings (no bare, hairy shins when you cross your legs here!) and black wingtip shoes. Or the female equivalent thereof.

But at some other company, it might mean a much more casual or radical dress code. The point is to bring with you the tools required to do the job, even if it's just an attitude that says, "Okay, I'm ready. Let the day's games begin!"

These notions may be somewhat shocking.

But they are the real secret of finding a job. Your co-authors have a combined total of over 40 years of work experience in many different jobs (government, private industry, and entreprenurial). And long ago, that experience taught us that simple competence is often all it takes to succeed.

There are so many drones out there who are just putting in their time and doing only enough to get by that you yourself don't have to be talented or gifted or extraordinarily intelligent. If you are simply *competent*—someone who wants to work, is willing to learn, and willing to show up on time, you *will* succeed.

That's what we mean when we advise you to take the initiative and show a little spark, some genuine interest, in a given position or company. At best, this simple step could give you the edge over your competition and land you the job. At worst, it's not going to *lose* you

the job, for the good companies really want people who are enthusiastic.

You certainly cannot limit your job search to the Internet and other online resources. But you should deal with all such resources and leads as part of an organized project or campaign. It will do you very little good to fire off a bunch of electronic resumes and forget about them.

Multimedia resumes: Fact or fallacy?

In its October 31, 1994, issue U.S. News & World Report *printed an article called "Your Credentials Plus a Song and Dance: Next time you update your resume, try adding sound and graphics."*

The article told the tale of one Jonathan Hudson, who graduated from Syracuse University with a B.F.A. in advertising design. Mr. Hudson had the brilliant idea of preparing a multimedia resume and sending it on disk to more than 75 advertising agencies and graphic design firms in Chicago, New York, and Philadelphia. The article reported that this generated "about 50 responses and 30 interviews. No job yet, but he has picked up some freelance work."

The article went on to affirm that "Hudson is one of a burgeoning number of job hunters updating their resumes for the 21st century by making them interactive and adding multimedia components. Employers seem wowed."

Well, maybe. But this approach seems 180 degrees at odds with the assertion of Los Angeles Times career columnist Joyce Lain Kennedy that companies are so beset with resumes that they are using scanners, OCR programs, and other software to dramatically reduce the amount of time a human resources manager must spend paging through resumes to make a "first cut."

So now we are to believe that these same time-pressed human resources managers are going to take the time to load an on-disk multimedia resume and spend 15 to 20 minutes clicking on icons that include not only text, but photographic, video, and sound components?

Well, maybe. If the job opening is for a multimedia programmer, it makes good sense to submit a multimedia resume as a sample of what you can do. And, of course, all the files needed for this can be packed into a single archive file and uploaded to an online system.

But the notion that a multimedia resume—complete with photos of the person, a sound clip or two explaining why he or she would make an outstanding hire, and an elaborate text file complete with hypertext links—will even approach the norm is preposterous.

Here's what Margaret Mannix, the US News reporter who wrote the article had to say:

> So far, these newfangled resumes are used mostly by people in computer-related occupations. But any professional who creates a product can make use of the technology. Photographers can feature their prints; architects can showcase their designs. Even furniture makers might consider displaying their masterpieces on a disk instead of in a brochure. And recent college graduates lacking in job history but rich in computer skills may get a leg up by showing their skills off in a multimedia resume.

Well, maybe, Ms. Mannix. But don't hold your breath. Just because something can be done in personal computing does not mean that it will become the norm. It only means that someone, somewhere, will do it. And, most of the time that someone will try to persuade a computer-illiterate mass media that it is the greatest thing since Ben and Jerry's ice cream. After all, who knows where the next computer-based fortune will be made? Who knows what the public will buy?

So far, at least, not even the Online Career Center has quite prepared itself for multimedia resumes. The U.S. News article reported in mid-October 1994 that "the Internet's Online Career Center, an employment database filled with 30,000 resumes, announced that job hunters can submit multimedia resumes via electronic mail. To get instructions, E-mail a request to **occ-info@occ.com** or call (317) 293-6499."

Several months after that article appeared, we sent a request to OCC asking for information about posting a multimedia resume. The message that came back read: "Sorry, but we are not ready to accept these resumes yet . . . It should be about 30 days."

We will leave you to make up your own mind about multimedia resumes. In our opinion, they are like the World Wide Web—an interesting sidelight, but something of far more smoke than genuine fire.

 # Purdue's Resume Workshop

Dave Taylor, creator of the Internet Mall and co-author with Rosalind Resnick of *The Internet Business Guide* (Sams Publishing), has also had a hand in developing the Purdue University Writing Lab and it's online version, the Online Writing Lab (OWL). Here are the various ways to gain access:

URL: **http://owl.trc.purdue.edu/**
Gopher: **owl.trs.purdue.edu**
FTP: **owl.trc.purdue.edu**
E-mail: **owl@sage.cc.purdue.edu** (Subject: "owl-request")

This is a wonderful service! For starters, it offers over 100 documents dealing with various aspects of writing, including writing resumes. Figure 15-1 shows the greeting screen you can expect when you access OWL via the World Wide Web. And Fig. 15-2 shows you the Web screen for the "Resume Workshop" feature.

Figure 15-1

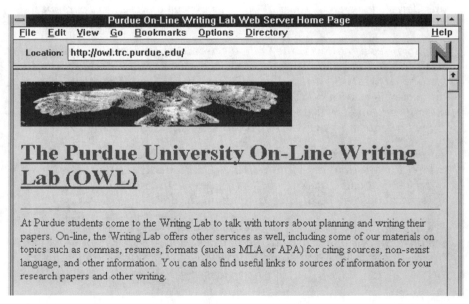

OWL's opening screen.

Figure 15-2

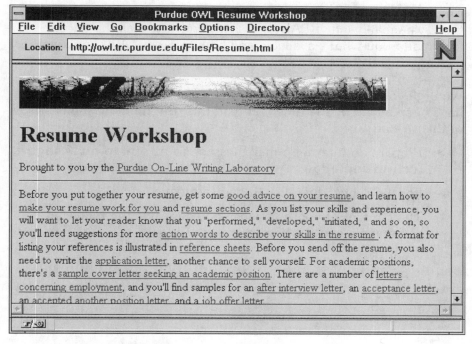

The OWL Resume Workshop feature.

⇨ The e-mail approach

Most of the files offered by OWL can also be gotten by sending a simple e-mail request. But first you've got to know the "number" of the file to request. And the quickest way to get that information is to FTP to **owl.trc.purdue.edu**. If you then key in dir, you will see a directory like this:

```
------r--    0     3362      3362 Oct 12 13:32 definitions
------r--    0     7437      7437 Nov 15 20:55 filelist
drwxr-xr-x       folder      11 Jan 15 17:15 handouts
------r--    0     1967      1967 Oct 25 22:00 help
------r--    0     1287      1287 Oct 12 15:04 How-to-Use-OWL-via-email
------r--    0     1353      1353 Oct 14 14:38 Introduction-to-OWL
------r--    0     7582      7582 Nov 20 15:00 Master-Index
------r--    0      973       973 Jan 15 17:02 Owl-via-Web-FTP-WORDS
------r--    0     5559      5559 Oct 25 22:00 README
------r--    0     1751      1751 Jan 15 17:02 USER-SURVEY
drwxr-xr-x       folder       1 Jan 15 17:15 Writing-Labs
```

There are at least two files you should be sure to get: "How-to-Use-OWL-via-email" and "README." They'll give you all the latest information on what's available and how to order OWL handouts for delivery to your Internet mailbox.

We urge you to try this yourself because new information is sure to have been added by the time you read this. But here are the basics as of this writing:

➢ Prepare an Internet e-mail message to be sent to **owl@sage .cc.purdue.edu**.

➢ For the subject line, key in owl-request.

➢ The content of your message should include the following commands, each on a separate line:

send 35
send 43
send 44
send 45
send 46
send 50
send 53
send 57
send 58
send 59

Here's a list of the documents you will soon find in your electronic mailbox:

Document 35—Your Resume...
Document 43—Letters Concerning Employment
Document 44—Accepted Another Position Letter (sample letter)
Document 45—After Interview Letter (sample letter)
Document 46—Cover Letter Seeking Academic Position (sample
                 letter)
Document 50—The Resume: Making it work for you
Document 53—Resume Sections
Document 57—Application Letters: How to Sell Yourself
Document 58—Accepted Another Position Letter (sample letter)

Document 59—Some Action Words used to Describe Skills in
    Resumes

But OWL goes further still. The good folks at Purdue University will
even help you *write* your resume—though, understandably, the needs
of Purdue students come first. Bottom line: You owe it to yourself to
try this site. In our opinion it is absolutely first class!

16

Making contacts

Newsgroups, mailing lists, & SIGs

CHAPTER 16

HOW'S this for a thesis:

> The *best* jobs never appear in the newspaper, online, on a recruiter's desk, or on a personnel agency's list. The best jobs are the ones you learn about through private, personal contacts.

Certainly, that statement doesn't apply in all situations. It may not even apply in a majority of situations. But no one who has *ever* looked for a job can deny that there is at least a kernel of truth to it. And we're not talking about some C.E.O. hiring her nephew or her husband's second cousin.

If you're new to the job-hunting game, what you've got to remember is that companies, government agencies, and other institutions with jobs to offer are staffed by human beings. As such, they tend to operate like other human organizations—clubs, societies, church groups, and so on. If there is one incontrovertible fact, it is that, regardless of the human organization, *relationships count!*

The problem for a job seeker is that the people with whom you want and need to establish a relationship—the people who can tip you off to upcoming openings or introduce you to valuable contacts or even offer you a job—are all on the inside. They're already members of the club. And you have no way to reach them to establish a relationship and show them what a fine person you are.

At least that used to be the case.

Today, many of the people you want to meet and get to know participate in what one might call "open clubs" online. These are the Internet newsgroups and mailing lists, and the Special Interest Groups (SIGs) you will find on commercial systems like CompuServe, Prodigy, and AOL. All of these terms are explained in Chapters 3, 4, and 6 of this book. So, if you have not yet read those chapters, you'd best go back and do so now. In *this* chapter, we're going to assume that you have done just that.

Is networking in or out?

For as long as we can remember, *networking* has been the buzzword. It was the process that was supposedly responsible for landing 80 percent of the jobs. In 1994, however, a bit of disagreement began to emerge.

On the one hand, you've got Kate Wendleton, career counselor and founder of the Five O'Clock Club, a nationwide network of job-strategy groups. In the April 5, 1994, issue of *USA Today*, Ms. Wendleton said that the way people really get jobs is by networking and contacting companies directly. Answering ads, talking to search firms, and looking for electronic job postings should apparently represent only 10 percent of your effort. "If it makes you feel like you're making progress, do it," Ms. Wendleton says, "But don't delude yourself into thinking that this is a real job search."

 # "Networking is dead!"

On the other hand, you've got William J. Morin, chairman of Drake Beam Morin, a large New York outplacement firm. As reported in the *Wall Street Journal* (November 22, 1994), Mr. Morin believes that, "Networking is dead! I know I'm saying something blasphemous, but there's a real backlash against networking because it's been so overworked."

In the same article, Michael E. McGill, chairman of the Organization Behavior Department at the Southern Methodist University business school said, "Networking is a bankrupt concept." And David B. Opton, of Exec-U-Net, a networking co-operative for senior executives said, "You get a call at work that feels like networking, and you want to throw up. "The illustration for this "Managing Your Career" article showed a frantic-looking person being chased by a telephone handset!

A different *kind* of networking

So, who's right? Is networking dead or is it still the best way to get the best jobs? The answer, in our opinion, is that both points of view are correct. The problem lies in what one means by *networking*.

In the age of downsizing

Those who proclaim the death of networking as a job search approach mean the kind of networking that was so fashionable in the 1980s. You know—the books and articles that urged you to talk to absolutely everyone you have ever known (and their uncles and cousins and aunts) to spread the word that you are on a job quest. When you find someone, according to the drill, you call them and ask for an "informational interview." No specific job need be involved. Your goal is simply to get inside, learn about a company from a friend of a friend of a friend, and hit the person up for additional people you can talk to in the company.

It's a nice theory. It may even have worked for a while. But not in the 1990s, where the corporate downsizing movement has forced everyone to work harder.

The people you most want to talk to at a company now no longer have the time to give you. Managers these days have to share secretarial staff and often even type their own letters and do their own filing. The last thing they want is for some distant acquaintance of the person they roomed with freshman year at college—whom they haven't seen in 20 years—to call and request an "informational interview."

High-tech ads worthless?

On the other hand, Ms. Wendleton is also correct when she says that the way people really get jobs is by networking and contacting companies directly. And full disclosure requires that we tell you that the October 11, 1994, "Labor Letter" feature on the front page of

the *Wall Street Journal* ran a squib titled "High-tech help wanteds flood online services but can be worthless." The squib included the following paragraph:

> Union Bank in Los Angeles fills only five openings through online ads, complaining they draw too many East Coast applicants. "I don't want to move the whole East Coast out here," says bank official Jim Ridings. Bernard Hodes Advertising, a recruiter, starts CareerMosaic, a talk, print, and graphics package, on the Internet. But a company public relations official fails to find anyone who got a job using the service.

⇨ The resolution & the answer

We don't mean to confuse you. But this is what people are saying. In our opinion, however, the answers are pretty simple.

High-tech ads and resumes are not worthless at all. The problem is that Union Bank and Bernard Hodes Advertising are victims of ridiculously inflated expectations. Someone probably told them that all they had to do was to put up a Web site and 20 million people would pay them a visit. As you know from previous chapters, we like both CareerMosaic and the Union Bank World Wide Web presence. These are quality operations.

The trouble is, the labor pool they want to tap is by and large far behind them on the technology curve. After all, at this writing, only 10 percent of Internet users have the ability to access the World Wide Web. So that's 2 or 3 million people, not 20 or 30 million. Of those 2 or 3 million, how many are likely to be job candidates? And of that subset, how many are likely to have heard about CareerMosaic and the Union Bank Web home page?

That the labor pool will catch up, we have no doubt. Indeed, we hope this book helps to accelerate the process. Clearly, to any thinking person, it is far too early to call these efforts a failure. These firms, and those like them, need to be patient, they need to constantly improve and test their Web or other offerings, and they've got to *advertise* their presence.

As for networking, in our opinion, for all the reasons cited earlier in this chapter, the 1980s' style of this activity is indeed dead. That's what makes the subject of this chapter so exciting. For, while that kind of networking may be defunct, Kate Wendleton is also correct in saying that *contacting people at companies* is the key.

That's where we come in.

Which is to say, that's where the Internet and the commercial online systems come in. They make it easy to do the kind of networking required for the 1990s. And in this chapter, we're going to show you how to do it!

Here's what to do

The September 1994 issue of *Online Access* carried a brief item titled "Another Kind of Network." The item reported that "Sometimes making the right connection with the right person in a context unrelated to jobs can make job-related things happen." It went on to recount the story of journalist and computer expert Daniel Browning, who was in CompuServe's journalism SIG and happened to answer a question posted by Jeff Krummer of the *St. Paul Pioneer Press*.

"Through e-mail, the two of them got to know each other fairly well. When a job opportunity for a computer-assisted reporting specialist with the St. Paul paper became available, Browning was offered—and eventually accepted—the job. This opportunity came as a result of his correspondence with Krummer."

The most powerful features of all

That's the kind of thing we're talking about in this chapter!

The job banks, resume postings, job listing services, World Wide Web sites, and everything else discussed in previous chapters are important. Indeed, they are *very* important. If they weren't, we wouldn't have told you about them. You will want to take full advantage of them, using the techniques we have presented.

But it's impossible to overemphasize the importance of the kind of networking we have just described. In our opinion, the most effective way to find a job using the Internet and other online services is to actively participate in the following features:

➤ Internet newsgroups

➤ Internet mailing lists

➤ Special Interest Groups (SIGs) on commercial systems

⇨ Level-setting: Before you begin

We're going to look at each of these three areas in turn. But before plunging in, we need a quick reality check. The first reaction most people experience on being fired or otherwise in need of a job is *panic*. Then you tell yourself, "I can deal with this. I can do it." You prepare a dynamite resume, send it out to four or five places, and make follow-up calls. And? . . . Nothing, nada, zip! . . . It's as if you don't exist. Desperation sets in.

We've been there, and we know. We also know that, unless your circumstances are extraordinary, there is no need for any hard-working individual to be desperate. Concerned, yes, of course. But not desperate. Thanks to the social safety net of unemployment insurance, food stamps, and the rest, you can at least survive.

There are two reasons why we're hitting this so hard, why we are so insistent that you calm down and convert your desperation to concern. First, desperation never brings out the best in a person. In general, we all tend to shy away from obviously desperate people. That's just human nature. So be confident in your worth and be cool—even if it means you've got to eat peanut butter sandwiches for dinner.

⇨ Ripening over time

Second, we want to emphasize the fact that human relationships need to ripen over time. You will never get to know someone in a

two- or three-message e-mail correspondence. And they will never get to know you. So start your online relationship-building early, well before you find yourself in a job search, if possible.

The surest way to drive yourself down is to sign onto an unfamiliar newsgroup or SIG the day after you're fired and post a message that begins, "Hi, all! I'm new. Has anybody heard of any job openings at bond-trading firms? If you have, you can message me at . . ."

If you're lucky, you'll get *flamed* by just one or two of the regular users—which means they will send you a nasty message suggesting all manner of anatomically impossible feats and calling into question your parents' marital status when you were born. If you're *very* lucky, no one will notice, and your message will "scroll off" into oblivion in a week or two with no further consequences.

 # Genuine communities

You know our background. You know how many books we've written about the online world over the past 12 years or so. Presumably you can conclude that we have some idea of what we are talking about when we say the mistake most new online users make is assuming that newsgroups, mailing lists, and SIGs are like a TV or radio call-in show. Which is to say, open to everyone with a telephone.

On the surface, that is indeed true. Anyone with a computer, a modem, and an account on a given system or access to the Internet can participate in the features discussed here. There is no one to stop you from uploading your own messages or your comments on messages uploaded by others.

But unlike *Larry King Live* or *Rush Limbaugh* or any of the other call-in programs you may encounter, online newsgroups, mailing lists, and SIGs are genuine *communities*.

⇨ How would *you* feel?

We implore you to think about this with us for just a moment, since it is the key to using these powerful features effectively.

Imagine that you and possibly your significant other bought a home in a brand-new housing development 20 years ago. You've seen neighbors come and go, but through it all, there is a core of people and families, many of whom were the "original settlers." This core consists of personalities who are liked, disliked, loved, and possibly hated. For better or for worse, everyone knows everyone else. These folks are a real community, and they have a history with one another.

That's what newsgroups, mailing lists, and SIGs are like. The community is by no means closed. New blood. New ideas. New people. All are truly welcomed. There are no barriers. After all, even if you wanted to do so, how can you tell a person's age, sex, size, or skin color when you're online? No one is going to stop you from buying a house in the development. No one is going to stop you from driving your van up and down the streets trying to sell your wares.

But you must never, ever forget that these entities are human *communities*. If you charge into—if you *invade*—such a community without due respect for its traditions, its leaders, and its way of doing things, you will get exactly what you deserve! In a word or two: Be humble and be deferential. Be aware that you are the outsider and the "newbie" as far as this community is concerned. Be aware that you will have to "earn" your acceptance—just as you would if you had joined a new swim club or community group.

⇨ How to work with newsgroups

There are some 10,000 Internet newsgroups devoted to every topic you can imagine. Messages posted to newsgroups flow through the Internet's cables and connections like the jetstream overhead. Not all sites on the Net "subscribe" to all newsgroups. The selection is up to the administrator of the site.

215

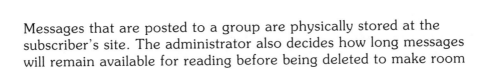
Messages that are posted to a group are physically stored at the subscriber's site. The administrator also decides how long messages will remain available for reading before being deleted to make room for new messages.

To read newsgroup postings, you will have to use a "newsreader" program. In the UNIX world, you are likely to find yourself using programs called *nn*, *trn*, or *tin*. Those, at least, are the old standbys, but many newer, easier programs have been developed in recent years.

On Delphi, for example, you have your choice of nn or the Delphi Navigator. (Pick Navigator. It is much, much easier to use than nn.) Netcom's Netcruiser and The Pipeline's software have built-in proprietary newsreaders. Or your Internet access provider may have supplied you with a shareware program like Trumpet for Windows or WinVN.

There is no need to get bogged down in the mechanics. Basically, if you are using a SLIP/PPP connection, Trumpet or WinVN or some other program based on your own computer can be told to automatically sign on, go to your favorite newsgroups, and pick up any new messages.

The program will then sign off and you will be free to read and prepare replies to newsgroup messages at your leisure. You can then tell the program to sign on again and transmit your replies to the appropriate areas automatically.

Job listings on a newsgroup

*Shown below is an online session in which we tapped into the newsgroup **biz.jobs.offered**. We used Delphi's Usenet newsreader program. Notice that the system reported a total of 1829 messages posted in the last 14 days—and notice that it knew we had read none of them.*

We opted to look at all unread messages. That produced a list of "discussion threads," presented in groups of 19 items at a time. There are two types of postings to a newsgroup: the initial posting and the replies. The initial posting begins the thread of messages. It opens the discussion, in effect. The replies (and replies to replies) that people

post constitute the elements of the discussion thread. Notice that Threads 11, 12, and 13 below each have three messages in their threads.

Since Thread 10 looked interesting, that's the one we opted to read. The text that was then displayed was a posting from TAD Data Services. Notice that TAD does not suggest you reply to this thread but that you use other means.

Finally, the Delphi newsreader, like all other newsreaders, keeps track of the threads and messages you have read. Thus, having read the TAD posting in this session, even if we were to leave the group and return a few seconds later, that thread would no longer appear on the menu of threads. All the threads would scroll up one place, with the former 11 becoming 10 and so on.

This is a real convenience, for it means you won't have to constantly review the same thread names each time you enter a group. And, in any case, you can change the default setting of "Unread" by opting to be shown "All" messages as you enter a group.

```
1829 messages have been posted in the last 14 days; You've read none of them.

Select which messages: Unread, All, Date or ?> [unread]
biz.jobs.offered

Page 1 of 84 [1829 messages in 1582 discussion threads]

   1   UNiSYS Corporation (available positions)
   2   STRATUS COMPUTER, INC. (available positions)
   3   Sales Agents Wanted!
   4   US-AZ We still have 10 positions open for UNIX/C applications progs
   5   Seeking Self-Starter in Las Vegas area...
   6   US-TX  Tech Support Mgr, Unix, Novell--Recruiter
   7   US-CA-LA video engineer BSEE, prod des, video SP,50mhz-1ghz; permanent
   8   US-CA-LA h/w design engineer BS/MSEE,RF/microwave,CAE; permanent
   9   US-CA-TUSTIN-SR P/A--Job Posting
  10   US-GA-Many Opportunities in Atlanta Area
  11   US-NJ-Homdel CDPD Cellular R&D Professionals, (3 msgs)
  12   US-MD-Laurel RF Systems Engineer,  3rd Party Recruiter (3 msgs)
  13   US-MD-Laurel Cellular Network Engineer,  3rd Party Recruiter (3 msgs)
  14   US-FL-SOUTH FLORIDA-SYSTEMS ANALYST, ROMAC
  15   US-NJ-CENTRAL NJ-PROJECT ENGINEER/MANAGER, ROMAC
  16   US-MID-WEST-CHEMIST, ROMAC17  Editorial Services
  18   US-FL-MAITLAND-ELECTRONIC DESIGNER, SYSTEM ONE
  19   US-FL-MIAMI-PROJECT MANAGER -STRUCTURAL, SYSTEM ONE

Enter Thread Number, MORE, PREV, ADD, ?, or EXIT: 10
```

```
[Message 1 of 1 in thread 10 of 1582] biz.jobs.offered

US-GA-Many Opportunities in Atlanta Area
    From: <tad_atlanta@interramp.com>
    Date: Sat, 21 Jan 95 16:28:28 PDT    (Page 1 of 1)
Data Services, a specialized division of TAD Resources
International is a nationwide organization with:

*    More than 38 years of uninterrupted growth
*    More than $800 million in annual sales
*    More than 20,000 employees
*    More than 240 offices worldwide
*    More than 1500 clients served

                NEW OPPORTUNITIES FOR 1995

20 + IMMEDIATE OPENINGS  IN THE ATLANTA, GA AREA

TECHNICAL SUPPORT SPECIALISTS with P.C. expertise. Individual
must be at expert level in one or more Microsoft products.
Position requires good communication skills. Will be working
with end users to solve their computer hardware and/or software
problems.

P.C. TECHNICIANS with experience troubleshooting and repair on
various computers. Ability to load software preferable.

NETWORK ADMINISTRATORS - UNIX, NCR 3000 platforms exp. Experience
in shell and C programming preferred. Understanding of Eudora
mail package, Starmail package.

For an immediate interview, forward your resume to:

TAD DATA SERVICES
4405 International Blvd.
Suite B-102
Norcross, Georgia  30093
Fax# 404-381-6601
Internet: tad_atlanta@interramp.com
```

Step-by-step instructions

Now let's look at the steps any job seeker should follow to make the most of Internet newsgroups. Start by looking at the nearby sidebar called "Job Listings on a Newsgroup." That will give you an idea of what you can expect.

 # Step 1: Identifying groups

Your first real step, however, is to identify the newsgroups you want to visit. See Chapter 4 of this book for instructions on obtaining the complete list of available newsgroups. As recommended there, put the list on your hard disk and search it with your word processor.

We did exactly that, searching on the word "jobs," and came up with the following two groups of newsgroups. The first grouping includes newsgroups likely to be of greatest interest to everyone, while the second grouping includes more specialized newsgroups:

biz.jobs.offered	Position announcements, business.
misc.jobs.offered	Announcements of positions.
available.misc.jobs.offered.entry	Job listings only for entry-level positions.
misc.jobs.resumes	Postings of resumes and "situation wanted" articles.
misc.jobs.contract	Discussions about contract labor.
misc.jobs.misc	Discussion about employment, workplaces, careers.
bionet.jobs	Scientific job opportunities (biology network).
bionet.jobs.wanted	Requests for employment in the biological sciences.
hepnet.jobs	High Energy Physics job announcements and discussions.
relcom.commerce.jobs	Jobs offered/wanted. (Russian language network.)
vmsnet.employment	VAX/VMS jobs sought/offered, workplace and employment-related issues. (Moderated)

Looking for newsgroups devoted to "jobs" or "resumes" or "employment" is an excellent first step. But keep in mind that there are many other groups devoted to most industries, professions, and interests. Use the "jobs" groups to get started. But plan to spend most of your time in the non-jobs groups since that's where you will find the kinds of people you want to meet and build relationships with.

Step 2: Resetting your counter

Until you've actually had some experience, you can't fully appreciate the vast quantities of text people post to the Net each day. Certainly no single newsgroup is visited by all 20 or 30 million Internet users. But tens of thousands of users is not out of the question. Not at all. And that can mean one whale of a lot of message traffic.

Thus, once you have identified a group of interest, Step 2 is to in effect reset your message counter. This is a two-part, one-time-only process. And it's easy.

Part One is to go to your target newsgroup. You will not have read any message threads, so all will be "new" to you. There very well may be a thousand or more threads, and, unfortunately, there is no way to search the thread names for items of interest when you are online. Therefore, do whatever your software requires to capture a list of thread topics to disk.

On Delphi, you need only open your comm program's capture buffer to record incoming text to disk. Then just keep hitting your Enter key until all the thread names have appeared. Look again at the sidebar presented earlier in this chapter and notice that some 84 pages are involved. So you would have to hit your Enter key 84 times to display all of the pages. A pain, yes, but you only have to do it once.

After you have captured all the thread titles to a disk file, sign off and bring that file into your word processor. There you can scroll through it at your leisure, making a note of the items of specific interest. Then all you have to do is sign back on, go to the same group, and capture just those items you have decided are of interest.

By doing this, you will have, in effect, digested all of the messages and threads on the newsgroup at this moment. You will have extracted the essence, at least as it applies to your situation and interests.

Part Two is to tell your newsreader software that you want it to consider all the messages currently posted to the board as "read." In other words, you tell your software that the next time you sign on to that newsgroup, you want it show you only those messages that have been posted since the last time you were there.

Once you do this, once you effectively "catch up" with a given newsgroup, the postings become much more manageable. You can then set your software to go in and get all of the messages that are "new" to you. No need to discriminate. If only a few score or even a hundred messages are involved, you can get them all and, once you are offline, discard those that are not of interest.

 # Step 3: Check early & often

The one caveat is that you've got to tap into such a newsgroup regularly. Every other day or so. If you don't, the number of messages "new" to you will quickly become unmanageable. And this assumes that you are just *reading* messages, not engaging in a discussion—in which case, checking in every day, even several times a day, is mandatory.

The old joke you hear on election day is "Be sure to vote early and often!" Something of the same approach applies to newsgroups. If you want to participate in a given newsgroup, you really do have to keep up. That means you've got to check for new messages every other day or so. As you can imagine, some groups are far more active than others, so the timing needed to keep current varies widely.

If things get out of hand, possibly because you've been busy or on vacation, just repeat the message counter resetting process. Keep in mind, however, that if you want to build a relationship with anyone, you have got to *be there* on a regular basis.

 # Step 4: Your own postings

So far, we've talked about the best way to find newsgroups of interest and to get started *reading* message threads. But what about making your own voice heard?

That, of course, is the payoff of the entire exercise. If you do nothing but read the messages posted by others, you become, in effect, a "lurker."

Like the human communities they are, Internet newsgroups live or die on the basis of member participation. New voices and fresh viewpoints are always welcome. But you will be much more warmly received if you have done your homework first.

That means taking the time to get a sense of the group. Follow the procedures we have suggested here to review the thread topics and messages of interest. Be patient enough to spend two weeks reading and keeping up with the flow of the discussion on a regular basis.

Then, and only then, will you be in a position to think about asking a question or making a comment of your own. After all, would you arrive late at a friend's house, sit down at the dinner table, and immediately begin talking—completely oblivious of the conversations that were in progress long before you arrived? Of course not! Newsgroups are no different.

Nor is there any guarantee that by participating in newsgroups you will find and develop a bond with someone who can help you in your current or future job search. But it is certainly worth a try. And, once again, while you should start with the jobs-related groups, you should probably spend most of your efforts on groups related to your interests or industry or profession.

As for the mechanics of posting a message, you will almost certainly have the opportunity to prepare a posting with your word processor, while you are offline. You will have to gauge each newsgroup for yourself, but, in general, keep your messages short and to the point. And make sure to save the text in plain ASCII format. You will then

be able to use your comm program or newsreader to upload the previously prepared file to the desired group at the proper time.

 # Internet mailing lists

Now let's turn our attention to Internet mailing lists. The main difference between a newsgroup and a mailing list is that newsgroups present you with a menu of messages from which you may pick and choose. A mailing list, in contrast, is more formal and far less interactive. It is basically a list of people and their e-mail addresses. Messages are posted to the list by sending a single message to a single address. The mailing list software at that address takes over and sends a copy of the message to the electronic mailbox of everyone on the list. In short, if you belong to a mailing list, you get every posting or message, whether you want it or not. And anyone who belongs to the list can post to it.

At first blush, this sounds quite interesting. And it is. But mailing lists are not an ideal means of interactive discussion and communication. They are like gigantic "party lines" in which everyone must listen to what everyone else is saying, whether they want to or not.

 # The Bitnet connection

Mailing lists exist largely because of Bitnet. Created in 1981 at the City University of New York (CUNY), Bitnet is a network linking over 1000 colleges and universities in over 40 countries around the world. Net lore has it that *Bit* stands for "Because It's Time" or "Because It's There."

Whatever. The main thing you have to remember about Bitnet — aside from its distinctly academic orientation—is that it is *incompatible* with the Internet. Mail can be exchanged between the two networks via gateway systems. But Bitnet uses a different set of protocols for distributing information.

And, unfortunately, Bitnet never developed the technology to make interactive, free-flowing, Internet-style newsgroups possible. Instead,

Bitnet developed an automated mailing list system that is broadly referred to as *Listserv*. That's why there are so many Bitnet mailing lists. With no newsgroups to use, mailing lists were the next best solution.

Getting into mailing lists

As discussed in Chapter 4, the two leading lists of mailing lists are the SRI and PAML lists. Obtaining copies of these lists should be your first step, whether you get them from Glossbrenner's Choice or from one of the sites presented in Chapter 4. Put them on your hard drive, bring them into your word processor, and search them for keywords like "jobs" or "employment," or some topic or industry of interest. Here, for example, is one of the "hits" we found when searching the PAML list on "job":

```
HTMARCOM

Contact: kimmik@bayne.com (Kim M. Bayne)

Purpose: To discuss High Tech MARketing COMmunications as it
relates to Computer and Electronics products and services and to
share information on resources available to High Tech
MARcommunicators. Level of discussion varies from basic how-to-
do-it to high-level marketing strategy in the Computer and
Electronics industries.

HTMARCOM posts a monthly online newsletter containing articles,
job listings, product reviews, media changes, conferences and
seminars. Resource lists and past newsletters are also available to list
subscribers in the HTMARCOM archives.

To subscribe send to: LISTSERV@usa.net
Message text: subscribe <listname> <Your Real Name>
```

How to subscribe to a mailing list

To get your name added to or removed from a mailing list, whether it originates on the Internet or on Bitnet, you send an e-mail message containing your request to a designated location. The SRI and PAML lists of mailing lists will give you the specifics of what to do to subscribe or unsubscribe. (Notice the "To subscribe" information presented as part of the PAML listing shown above.)

Not every set of instructions is equally complete. The points to zero in on are these:

> ➤ Where should the subscription request be sent?

> ➤ What, specifically, should the message contain?

> ➤ Where should actual contributions to the list—as opposed to subscription requests—be sent.

Some mailing lists are completely automated—your subscription request is read by and acted upon by a computer. Other lists are managed by a human being, in which case you subscribe by sending that person a short note. Read the mailing list subscription information carefully to determine which is the case for any list you want to subscribe to. Then be sure to send your request to the "subscription-request" address (*not* to the address used for posting messages).

Finally, if you subscribe to several very active mailing lists, you might want to consider unsubscribing before going away on a long vacation. It's a simple enough matter, and can save you from coming home to a mailbox jammed with messages you may not have time to wade through. Just add it to your "travel checklist" along with stopping the regular mail and newspaper deliveries.

How to subscribe to an automated list

*Some mailing lists, especially those on Bitnet, are managed by a machine running some kind of "list management" program. The main programs or list managers are LISTSERV, MAJORDOMO, and LISTPROC. Thus, to subscribe to a particular mailing list, you might be told to send your request to an address like **listserv@host.site** or **majordomo@host.site** or **listproc@host.site**.*

You will want to verify the specific requirements for each list, but in general, all you have to do is include a line in the following format in your message to the automated list server:

```
subscribe listname your_name
```

In this case, your_name *is your first name and last name, not your network e-mail address. Leave the subject line in your message blank since it will be ignored anyway.*

 # Special Interest Groups (SIGs)

As we have been saying in print for the last dozen years or so, Special Interest Groups (SIGs) are the best reason for *anyone* to go online. Shopping, e-mail, interactive multi-player games, chat, and the like are great. But, in our opinion, SIGs are where it's at. This feature goes by different names—a Forum on CompuServe, a RoundTable (RT) on GEnie, a Club or Bulletin Board (BB) on Prodigy or America Online, and a SIG on Delphi. But the concept is the same.

SIGs are essentially online clubs or organizations devoted to some particular interest. They exist only on commercial systems like America Online, CompuServe, Prodigy, Delphi, GEnie, and the rest, and they are typically profit-making enterprises. That means that the person in charge—the *sysop* or *system operator*—is paid a percentage of the connect time charges accumulated by subscribers while they are using the SIG.

Thus, the goal of *every* SIG sysop on *every* system is to create and maintain a feature that will be so good, so useful, so helpful, and so entertaining that users will gladly spend lots of time using it. In short, unlike Internet newsgroups, commercial system SIGs are managed by one or more individuals who have a financial incentive to do a really good job.

In addition, SIGs were designed from the ground up to facilitate the exchange of information among people, whether it be public messages, private messages, files, or real-time conversation and chat. And over the past decade or so, they developed independently of the Internet's newsgroups and mailing lists. After all, until just a few years ago, no one but academics, defense contractors, and Pentagon people could get access to the Internet.

 ## A crude alternative

All of which is a gentle way of saying that Internet newsgroups and mailing lists are terribly crude when compared to the SIGs on systems like CompuServe and AOL. You will want to cover all bases as you

seek kindred souls or people at companies with whom you can establish relationships. But don't neglect the commercial systems discussed first in Part 1 of this book.

Each of these systems has a role to play, but if you want to meet the kinds of people who may eventually be able to hire you, you should probably start with CompuServe. Delphi has some great features and some great SIGs, but its main claim to fame at this writing is fast, complete, text-based access to the Internet.

Keep in mind that in this field things can change overnight. As of this writing, however, AOL and Prodigy are neat systems, but they are very "home-oriented" and thus not the best spots to encounter potential contacts and employers. As for GEnie, well, due to corporate neglect, it has very little to offer anyone at this time, sad to say.

 # The basic SIG floorplan

Two things are required to take best advantage of what we feel is a remarkable set of resources. First, you've got to get a list of all the SIGs on a given system. That means using the system's features that let you search or capture its entire keyword list. Once the list is captured as a text file on your disk, you can print it out or search it at leisure. (See Chapter 6 for specific instructions on getting a list of keywords from each commercial system.)

After you have identified the Clubs or BBs or SIGs or Forums or whatever that are of greatest interest, the next step is to pay them a visit and get a sense of what they are all about. (Hint: Tell your comm program to capture all incoming text to a file *before* you enter a SIG for the first time.)

If you are asked to "join" a SIG, do so. We can think of no SIG that imposes any costs or membership fees. But on CompuServe, for example, if you do not "join" a SIG—a simple matter of keying in your name—you may not be permitted to download files from the SIG libraries.

 # The main "rooms" of any SIG

"Libraries?" What do you mean by "libraries?"

We're happy to explain. Entering a SIG is like strolling into a fraternity or sorority house on a college campus. You walk in and find a message board on your right where members post information and questions about tickets wanted or for sale, rides to distant colleges or home, and so on.

As you walk down the entrance hall toward the staircase, you notice members engaged in discussions of various topics in the rooms to your right and left. You go up the stairs to the club library, a room divided into several alcoves. The books, programs, and other materials in each alcove are devoted to one particular aspect of the topic that is the main focus of the club.

In a club devoted to health and nutrition, for example, there might be alcoves in the library for files containing information about vitamins, weight-loss diets, exercise, and so on.

This is a far cry from the dumb "piano rolls" of messages posted to Internet newsgroups. In the commercial online world, all true online SIGs have three main components:

> ➢ A message board for the posting and answering of questions. To make it easy to locate messages of interest, most boards are divided into several topic or subject areas. As on the Internet, a message and a series of replies and replies-to-replies is called a *thread*.

> ➢ A conference area for real-time discussions and chat and guest speakers.

> ➢ A library offering software, text files, transcripts of club conferences with guest speakers, and particularly outstanding message threads.

Putting it all together

This chapter is designed to show you the *possibilities* that exist for anyone who wants to go beyond the job and resume listings discussed in the previous chapters. As such, it may be the most important chapter in the book. It all depends on your situation.

The fact of the matter is that if you have high-tech skills and job experience, you may very well find the ideal job using the features described in previous chapters. But if you are a liberal arts major or someone just starting out, you may do better working the newsgroups, mailing lists, and SIGs as discussed here.

 # Here's what to do

The most logical procedure to follow is this:

> ➤ Get a list of what's available, whether it's Internet newsgroups or mailing lists or the SIGs on commercial systems.

> ➤ Search that list or lists for topics or keywords of interest.

> ➤ Sign on to the relevant system and go to each feature of interest in turn. Do whatever you must to be sure of capturing all incoming text to disk as a text file that you can read or print out later.

> ➤ Stop. Take the time necessary to get to know the SIG, the newsgroup, the mailing list, or whatever.

> ➤ When you have what a public speaker would call "a sense of the house," offer a short comment or question, as appropriate.

> ➤ Check in every day. Eventually people will start commenting on your comments or otherwise begin a dialog. Respond to all comments and criticisms thoughtfully, reasonably, and with every other virtue you can think of.

Remember that your main purpose here is not necessarily to debate the issues but to present yourself to the community as a reasonable, well-spoken, thoughtful person.

Be honest. Be yourself. Be forceful about subjects or topics you believe in. But take your time and think before you type. Prepare and edit your postings offline, if you can. Which is to say, don't fly off the handle—ever. Assume that everything you write may be read by your future employer.

 # Managing your time

There's a popular T-shirt slogan that goes, "So many [blank], and so little time!" It doesn't matter whether you substitute for "[blank]" the word "porcupines" or "job search options," the statement still holds true.

There are so very many options—so many ways to pursue your quest—yet there are still only 24 hours in a day. Which options should you choose? Your co-authors have absolutely no idea! After all, we have no way of knowing your particular situation.

What we do know, however, is that Internet newsgroups and mailing lists and the SIGs on commercial systems can be tremendous assets in any job quest. But you can't bomb into them the day after you become unemployed and expect someone to offer you a job.

They don't know you, and you don't know them, after all. They don't care that you're in a panic, that you're desperate, that you've got three kids to feed. You're just one person in 20 or 30 *million*. No one knows you. No one's heard of you. And, frankly, no one has any reason to care about you.

Start today!

Unless you've got a track record at a high-tech company or can boast of some high-tech skill (like C++ programming, Novell network management, or HTML Web page creation), you are just a person.

Which is fine, but not terribly helpful when you are looking for a job. That's why you've got to start *now*—before you really need a job. You've got to move from being a mere "person" to being a

personality. Or at least to being a recognizable "presence" in your targeted newsgroups and SIGs.

Follow the logic. All human organizations, whether they are companies or clubs, are based on relationships. The Internet and commercial systems offer you the opportunity to establish relationships with people via newsgroups, mailing lists, and SIGs. But building relationships between or among human beings takes time.

There is no way around this. Nor should there be. Ideally, you would want to participate on a newsgroup, mailing list, or SIG out of sheer enthusiasm and interest in the topic. Not because of some future plans for landing a new job.

Six months from now—after you have established yourself as a giving, caring, enthusiastic member of the group—some member may signal you that there is a job opening for someone of your capabilities. Well, then, that's perfect.

Any number of scenarios are possible. The point is that newsgroups, mailing lists, and SIGs can be powerful tools in learning about job openings and in getting job offers. But they are not "instant" tools. If you hope to use them tomorrow, you must begin participating today!

The amount of time you spend on this activity is entirely up to you, of course. And make no mistake, whether you use the Internet or some commercial system, this *is* a time-consuming activity. Only you can decide how much time to devote to participating in Internet newsgroups and mailing lists and the SIGs offered by commercial systems.

But you should definitely explore *all* alternatives. On a job search, you should leave no stone unturned, after all.

Joining professional & trade organizations

CHAPTER 17

NOW let's turn to an often under-used job-finding technique—taking advantage of professional organizations and trade associations. If Internet newsgroups and SIGs on commercial systems are *de facto* communities and associations, the entities discussed here are the real thing.

There are societies and official organizations of one kind or another devoted to just about any activity or endeavor you can imagine. For proof, you need only pay a call on your friendly reference librarian at your nearest library and ask where you can find a book called *The Encyclopedia of Associations.* You'll discover over 88,000 nonprofit membership organizations described in its pages.

In our opinion, every job seeker—and certainly every college student or anyone looking for that first job—should spend an hour with *The Encyclopedia of Associations.* And don't be shy about contacting organizations of interest. Supplying information on an industry or profession is one of the main reasons associations exist in the first place.

 # Checking it online

If you have access to a DIALOG account, the Encyclopedia of Associations database is File 114 on that system. But at a connect-time rate of $108 an hour ($1.80 a minute), searching that database can be an expensive activity. You'll probably be better off checking at your local library.

Fortunately, there is a ton of information about associations, societies, and the like on the Internet. There are two main places to check: The University of Waterloo's Scholarly Societies Project, and the Millsaps College (Jackson, Mississippi) Gopher.

 # The Scholarly Societies Project

The library at Canada's University of Waterloo has created a Gopher that provides links to Gophers and other servers of scholarly

societies. Societies like the American Philosophical Association, the Association for Computing Machinery (ACM), and Institute for Electrical and Electronics Engineers (IEEE).

Societies here isn't as stuffy as it sounds. The library uses the word to mean organizations in which membership is "determined by scholarly credentials, not by the existence of a contract of employment or of visitation rights, as in the case of a research centre." A society will typically have a word like "Society," "Association," "Union," or "Institute" in its name.

As you can see from Figs. 17-1 and 17-2, you can use this feature via the World Wide Web. Simply load your Web browser and open the URL **http://www.lib.uwaterloo.ca/society/overview.html**. You will find the site interesting, to be sure, but you will probably find the Gopher implementation to be more useful.

Figure **17-1**

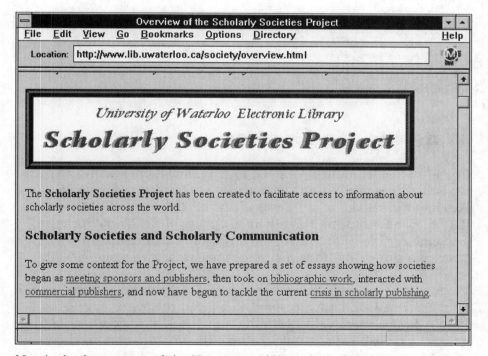

Here's the first screen of the University of Waterloo's Scholarly Societies Project on the World Wide Web. It's designed to give you an overview of the feature.

235

Figure 17-2

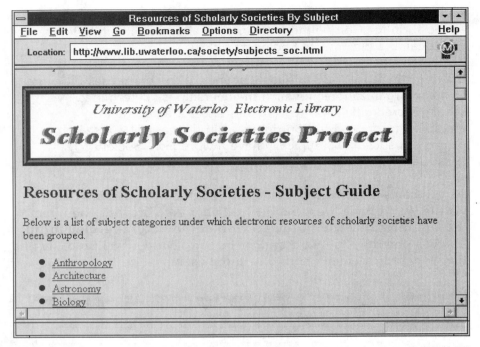

As you can gather, this screen organizes the Project's resources by subject of which there are over 30.

⇨ Waterloo via Gopher

To get to this feature via Gopher, specify the Gopher address **watserv2.uwaterloo.ca**. Then choose "Electronic Resources Around the World," then "Campus and other information systems (CWIS, gophers, BBS)," and then "Gophers of Scholarly Societies." See Fig. 17-3 for currently covered societies, and check this site on your own since new Gopher connections are always being added.

When you select an item from the menu shown in Fig. 17-3, you will be taken to a Gopher maintained by a given society or association. What you find there varies with the organization, of course. But in general, you can expect to learn about the organization and how to join, a calendar of meetings, lists of publications, FTP sites and archives, links to Gophers of related interest, and so on.

Gophers of Scholarly Societies

Figure 17-3

```
Page 1 of 1
1    About the Scholarly Society Gophers area                      Text
2    Composite Link File for the Scholarly Society Gophers area    Text
3    FLASH! Much Enhanced WWW Version Now Available                Text
4    Academy of Finland Gopher                                     Menu
5    Academy of Management (Management Archive)                    Menu
6    Akademie Ved, CR (Academy of Sciences, Czech Republic) Gophe  Menu
7    American Academy of Veterinary Informatics (AAVI) Gopher      Menu
8    American Association for the Advancement of Core Curriculum    Menu
9    American Association for the Advancement of Science (AAAS) G   Menu
10   American Association of Immunologists (AAI) Gopher            Menu
11   American Association of Teachers of French (AATF) Gopher      Menu
12   American Astronomical Society (AAS) Gopher                    Menu
13   American Chemical Society (ACS) Gopher                        Menu
14   American Educational Research Association                     Menu
15   American Folklore Society (AFS) Gopher                        Menu
16   American Geological Institute (AGI) Gopher                    Menu
17   American Indian Science and Engineering Society (AISES) Goph  Menu
18   American Institute of Physics (AIP) Gopher                    Menu
19   American Library Association (ALA) [BIG] Gopher               Menu
20   American Library Association (ALA) [smaller] Gopher           Menu
21   American Mathematical Society (AMS) Gopher                    Menu
22   American Medical Writers Association (AMWA) Gopher            Menu
23   American Meteorological Society Gopher                        Menu
24   American Philological Association (APA) Gopher [Transactions  Menu
25   American Philosophical Association Gopher                     Menu
26   American Physiological Society Gopher                         Menu
27   American Political Science Assocation Gopher                  Menu
28   American Psychological Association (APA) [Psycoloquy only]    Menu
29   American Psychological Society (APS) Gopher                   Menu
30   American Society for Cell Biology (ASCB) Gopher               Menu
31   American Society for Histocompatibility and Immunogenetics (  Menu
32   American Society for Investigative Pathology (ASIP) Gopher    Menu
33   American Society for Pharmacology and Experimental Therapeut  Menu
34   American Society of Zoologists (ASZ) Gopher                   Menu
35   American Studies Association (ASA) Gopher                     Menu
36   American Veterinary Computer Society (AVCS) Gopher            Menu
37   Animal Behaviour Society (ABS) Gopher                         Menu
38   Applied Anthropology Computer Network (ANTHAP)                Menu
39   Arbeitsgemeinschaft Simulation (ASIM) Gopher                  Menu
40   Association for Computing Machinery (ACM) Gopher              Menu
41   Association for Educational Communications & Technology Goph  Menu
42   Association for Public Policy Analysis and Management (APPAM  Menu
43   Association for Supervision and Curriculum Development (ASCD  Menu
44   Association for Women Geoscientists Gopher                    Menu
45   Association for the Advancement of Computing in Education (A  Menu
46   Association of American University Presses (AAUP) Gopher      Menu
```

Here is the complete list of items currently on the Scholarly Societies Gopher. But be sure to check this location yourself, since new Gopher links are always being added.

237

```
47  Association of Biomolecular Resource Facilities (ABRF) Gophe    Menu
48  Association of Research Libraries (ARL) Gopher                  Menu
49  Association of Universities and Colleges of Canada (AUCC) Go    Menu
50  Australian Computer Society Gopher                             Menu
51  British Computer Society Gopher                                Menu
52  CAUSE Gopher (information resources in higher education)       Menu
53  California Academy of Sciences Gopher                          Menu
54  Canadian Information Processing Society (CIPS) National Goph    Menu
55  Canadian Mathematical Society  (CMS) Gopher                    Menu
56  Canadian Society for Theoretical Biology (CSTB) Gopher         Menu
57  Cliometric Society Economic History Server                     Menu
58  Czech & Slovak Simulation Society (CSSS) Gopher                Menu
59  Czech Academy of Sciences (Prague) Gopher                      Menu
60  Dutch Benelux Simulation Society (DBSS) Gopher                 Menu
61  European Association for Computer Graphics (Eurographics)      Menu
62  European Association for International Education (EAIE) Foru    Menu
63  European Association of Distance Teaching Universities Gophe    Menu
64  European Chapter of the American Society for Information Sci    Menu
65  Federation of American Scientists                              Menu
66  Federation of American Societies for Experimental Biology (F    Menu
67  Federation of European Simulation Societies (EUROSIM) Gopher    Menu
68  Hume Society                                                   Menu
69  Hungarian Simulation Tools and Application Group (HSTAG) Gop    Menu
70  Industrial Computing Society (ICS) Gopher                      Menu
71  Institute of Electrical & Electronics Engineers (IEEE) Gophe    Menu
72  Institute of Management Sciences (TIMS) Gopher                 Menu
73  Institute of Physics (IP) Gopher                               Menu
74  Inter-Society for the Electronic Arts (ISEA) Gopher            Menu
75  International Association for Statistics Education (IASE) Go    Menu
76  International Association of Learning Labs (IALL) Gopher        Menu
77  International Association of Technology Assessment... (IATAF    Menu
78  International Association of Universities (IAU) Gopher          Menu
79  International Astronomical Union (IAU) Gopher                   Menu
80  International Council on Monuments and Sites (ICOMOS) Gopher    Menu
81  International Federation for Information Processing (IFIP) G    Menu
82  International Federation of Automatic Control (IFAC) Gopher     Menu
83  International Federation of Library Associations & Instituti    Menu
84  International Institute for Applied Systems Analysis (IIASA)    Menu
85  International Medical Informatics Association (IMIA)            Menu
86  International Research Group on Ostracoda (IRGO) Gopher         Menu
87  International Society for Knowledge Organization (ISKO), FFM    Menu
88  International Society for Neuroethology (ISN) Gopher            Menu
89  International Society for Technology in Education (ISTE) Gop    Menu
90  International Telecommunication Union (ITU) Gopher              Menu
91  International Telecommunications Society (ITS) Gopher           Menu
92  International Union Against Cancer (IUAG) Gopher                Menu
93  International Union of Crystallography (IUCr) Gopher            Menu
94  Internet Society (includes IETF) Gopher                        Menu
95  Italian Association for Artificial Intelligence (AI*IA) Goph    Menu
```

Figure 7-3. Continued.

```
96   Italian Society for Computer Simulation (ISCS) Gopher      Menu
97   Law and Society Association (LSA) Gopher                   Menu
98   Mathematical Association of America (MAA) Gopher           Menu
99   Middle East Studies Association                           Menu
100  Music Library Association (MLA) Gopher                    Menu
101  Mycological Society of America Bulletin Board             Menu
102  Operations Research Society of America (ORSA) Gopher      Menu
103  Paleontological Society                                   Menu
104  PanAmerican Society for Pigment Cell Research (PASPCR) Gophe  Menu
105  Peace Studies Association (PSA) Gopher                    Menu
106  Physiological Society Bulletin Board                      Menu
107  Rhizosphere Studies Working Group Gopher                  Menu
108  Societe de Simulation Francophone (FRANCOSIM) Gopher      Menu
109  Society for Electronic Access (SEA) Gopher                Menu
110  Society for Experimental Biology (SEB) Gopher             Menu
111  Society for Industrial & Applied Mathematics (SIAM) Gopher   Menu
112  Society for Mathematical Biology (SMB) Gopher             Menu
113  Society for Music Theory                                  Menu
114  Society for Neuroscience                                  Menu
115  Society for the Study of Symbolic Interaction (SSSI) Gopher  Menu
116  Turkish Academy of Sciences (TUBA) Gopher                 Menu
117  United Kingdom Simulation Society (UKSS) Gopher           Menu


Enter Item Number, SAVE, ?, or BACK:
```

 # The Millsaps Gopher

The other site you must not fail to visit is the Millsaps Gopher. The
Gopher address is **gopher.millsaps.edu**. Here's the menu you will
see:

```
gopher.millsaps.edu Gopher
Page 1 of 1


1    About... (05-Oct-1994)                                   Text
2    Computer Use Policies                                    Menu
3    Millsaps College Campuswide Information System (CWIS)    Menu
4    Jackson, Mississippi Area Information                    Menu
5    World-Wide Information - Access the Internet             Menu
6    Technical Information about the Millsaps Gopher Server   Menu


Enter Item Number, SAVE, ?, or BACK: 5
```

As you can see, we selected Item 5, "World-Wide Information - Access the Internet." That leads to a menu from which we chose "Internet Resources (new services, collections, etc.)." And that selection leads to a menu from which we chose "Selected Internet Resources (via Millsaps CDIAC)." You will then see a menu like this:

```
Selected Internet Resources (via Millsaps CDIAC)
Page 1 of 1

1    About...                                                    Text
2    Alliances, Consortiums, and Networks                       Menu
3    Books|Journals|Magazines|Newsletters|Newspapers            Menu
4    Bulletin Boards                                            Menu
5    Calendar, Time, and Weather Services                       Menu
6    Civil Liberties Organizations                              Menu
7    Commercial Services                                        Menu
8    Dictionaries, Glossaries and Thesauri                      Menu
9    Discussion Lists, Interest Groups                          Menu
10   Government Information Resources                            Menu
11   Grant and Funding Opportunities                            Menu
12   Guides - Gopher, Internet, Network Guides                  Menu
13   Hobbies, Leisure, Recreation, Travel, and Interesting Tidbit Menu
14   Internet Resources - Arranged by Subject                   Menu
15   Internet Resources - Virtual Reference Desks               Menu
16   Network Addresses - Find                                   Menu
17   Personal Computer Software - Public Domain and Shareware   Menu
18   Professional Societies and Organizations                   Menu

Enter Item Number, SAVE, ?, or BACK: 18
```

Choose "Professional Societies and Organizations" as we have done here, and you will see a menu of professional societies and organizations like the one shown here.

```
Professional Societies and Organizations
Page 1 of 1

1    About...                                                    Text
2    ANet, The Int'l Accounting Network (Australia) (Unsupported)
3    Academy of Management (Management Archive)                 Menu
4    American Association for the Advancement of Core Curriculum Menu
5    American Association of Zookeepers                          Menu
6    American Astronomical Society Gopher                        Menu
7    American Chemical Society                                   Menu
8    American Geological Institute                               Menu
9    American Heart Association                                  Menu
10   American Institute of Physics (AIP)                        Menu
```

```
11   American Mathematical Society (AMS)                         Menu
12   American Meteorological Society Gopher                      Menu
13   American Philosophical Association Gopher                   Menu
14   American Physiological Society                              Menu
15   American Political Science Assocation Gopher                Menu
16   American Psychological Society                              Menu
17   American Society for Cell Biology (ASCB) Gopher             Menu
18   American Society of Zoologists (ASZ) Gopher                 Menu
19   Association for Computer Machinery                          Menu
20   Association for Educational Communications & Technology     Menu
21   Association for Experiential Education (AEE) (Unsupported)
22   CAUSE Gopher                                                Menu
23   Conference and Seminar Announcements                        Menu
24   DECUS Gopher (Digital Equipment Corp User Group)            Menu
25   Educom                                                      Menu
26   Federation of American Societies for Experimental Biology (F  Menu
27   Gophers of Scholarly Societies via U. of Waterloo, CA       Menu
28   International Society for Technology in Education            Menu
29   Internet Society (includes IETF) Gopher                     Menu
30   Law and Society Association                                 Menu
31   Mathematical Association of America                         Menu
32   National Academy of Sciences (Unsupported)
33   National Association of College Broadcasters                Menu
34   National Institute of Health Gopher                         Menu
35   National Science Foundation Gopher                          Menu
36   Paleontological Society                                     Menu
37   Society for Music Theory                                    Menu


Enter Item Number, SAVE, ?, or BACK:
```

⇨ A Millsaps example

As with the Waterloo Scholarly Societies Project, there is no way to know beforehand what you will encounter when you select an item from the Millsaps Gopher shown previously. However, the Mathematical Association of America, Item 31 on that Gopher menu, illustrates how very good this feature can be. Here's the menu you will see when you select that item:

```
Mathematical Association of America
Page 1 of 1    .


1   About the MAA organization and its activities              Menu
2   Celebrating progress in collegiate mathematics             Menu
```

```
3    Committees and governance of the MAA                    Menu
4    Electronic services of other mathematical organizations Menu
5    General information of interest to mathematicians        Menu
6    Meetings calendar                                        Menu
7    Publications of the MAA                                   Menu
8    Sections of the MAA and their activities                 Menu
9    Student information and activities                       Menu
10   Women and Minorities                                     Menu
11   Mathematics Awareness Week --- 23-29 April 1995          Menu
12   Professional Development Activities                      Menu
13   Suggestion Box                                           Text
14   What's new on the MAA Gopher (January 1995)              Menu

Enter Item Number, SAVE, ?, or BACK:
```

Choosing "About the MAA organization and its activities" leads to a menu like this. Notice that the fourth item is "Employment Resources," which is indeed the item we picked:

```
About the MAA organization and its activities
Page 1 of 1

1    About the MAA                                Text
2    About the MAA Gopher+ Server                 Menu
3    Books of the MAA                             Text
4    Employment Resources                         Text
5    MAA Awards                                   Menu
6    MAA Headquarters Staff                       Text
7    MAA Membership Application                   Text
8    MAA Special Projects                         Text
9    National MAA officers available as speakers  Text
10   National Officers of the MAA                 Text
11   Policy documents and reports                 Menu
12   Polya Lectures                               Text
13   Sections of the MAA                          Text
14   Visiting Lecturers and Consultants           Text

Enter Item Number, SAVE, ?, or BACK: 4

Employment Resources
Page 1 of 1

THE MATHEMATICAL SCIENCES EMPLOYMENT REGISTER

In an effort to establish communications between
mathematical scientists available for employment and
employers with positions to fill, the American
Mathematical Society (AMS), the Mathematical Association
of America (MAA), and the Society for Industrial and
Applied Mathematics (SIAM), founded the Mathematical
Sciences Employment Register (MSER).
```

```
At the January Joint Mathematics Meetings an Employment
Register is maintained which lists brief precis of positions
available in the mathematical sciences. Interviews are
scheduled by computer between applicants and prospective
employers. Both applicant and employer must register for
the meeting and pay the regular meeting fee in order to
take advantage of the services of the Register. There is an
additional fee for applicants and employers participating in
the Register.

(etc.)
```

 # Conclusion

There is simply no question but that official societies, associations, and organizations can be a very valuable resource to anyone searching for a job. At the very least, they can provide you with information about a given industry or profession. But, as we've seen here, they can often provide much more.

These organizations, in short, offer yet another way to "get inside." No one's going to hand you anything on a silver platter. But with imagination, enthusiasm, and energy, you may find that professional societies, trade organizations, and associations can show you the way to the job you want. And the fact that so many of these groups offer so much information via the Internet makes it all the easier.

Online databases

More information

WE have laid a great deal of information before you in the previous 17 chapters. So much information, in fact, that you have good reason to feel a bit overwhelmed. And now here we go with a final chapter that's about . . . information. No one can blame you for asking whether this new topic is strictly necessary.

The answer is a strong "yes" and "no." Or better still, a ringing, "It all depends." We have made it our practice throughout this book to bring you only the best. In an old-fashioned sort of way, we figure that's what you're paying us for. This chapter is no exception. We're about to tell you about some really powerful online information tools that most career books simply overlook, probably because their authors are not aware of them.

Feeling the power

These tools are *commercial databases* like Standard & Poor's, Dun's Market Identifiers, Moody's Corporate Profiles, and Disclosure. Yet they are but a few of the thousands of databases you can tap to develop job leads; identify executives; and learn about companies, industries, professions, or any other field of endeavor.

Consider: At this very moment you may know absolutely nothing about magazine publishing, plastics, or plumbing supplies. But 24 hours from now, you can be an expert. Or at least you can know enough to be able to ask the right questions of someone interviewing you for a job in any of those industries.

You'll know the company's position in the industry, who its major competitors are, how experts feel about the future of the company and the industry as a whole, what the major issues are, the names and backgrounds of the major personalities, and whether or not the person interviewing you has been quoted recently in a newspaper or trade publication.

Rolling over your competition

That's the kind of power that online databases give you. And "power" really is the right word. Imagine, for example, two recent college graduates who are equal in every way. They are interviewing for the same job at a company. Who do you think is going to be more impressive: the person who expresses an interest in working there because he or she has "heard good things about" the company, or the person who has done the necessary research to have the kind of knowledge discussed here? There is simply no contest.

Your database-derived background isn't going to make you an expert on the company, of course. But that's not really what you're after. And you're certainly not going to fool anyone at the firm.

The purpose of the exercise is to demonstrate *interest*. So you don't have to be a "talker and dancer." Plain sincerity will do quite nicely. Recruiters, interviewers, and executives don't have to know that your knowledge was acquired electronically during the previous 24 hours. And you don't have to tell them.

What they will see is someone who, by golly, was interested enough in this company to take the time and effort to learn something about it and its industry. That's the kind of energetic, resourceful go-getter they can use in their organizations.

The knowledge you glean from online databases won't get you the job. As we all know, many, many factors are involved. But there is simply no question that this kind of information will give you an edge over most of your competitors. And, unlikely as it may be, should any of those competitors be smart enough to have done their homework too, you will at least be able to meet them as equals.

 # How to search a database

The answer to the question "How does one search a database?" Having written extensively about the subject (*How to Look It Up*

Online and *The Information Broker's Handbook*), we can say with conviction that searching online electronic databases is an art that can only be learned with practice.

If you are a master of that art, then by all means do it yourself. Indeed, if you're a student or someone else with free access to commercial online systems, take a stab at it. But if you must pay for the information, remember that searching is not a skill you can hope to master overnight, the way you might knock out a term paper or cram for a test.

That's why it's comforting to know that there are skilled professionals who can do it for you. If you've got more time than money, ask your local or college librarians if there is anyone on staff who's a crackerjack "Dialog, Nexis, or Dow Jones searcher." You may find that database searching is a service your library actually offers its patrons, though we've yet to find one that publicizes this fact. Typically, no labor charge will be involved; you will pay only the database charges.

 # Hire an information broker

If you are in a hurry or can otherwise afford to spend one to two hundred dollars for the service, an information broker can do the job and deliver the information overnight. Information brokers are the "hired guns" of the information industry. Tell them what you want, respond to their questions as they conduct a "reference interview" with you to bring things into sharper focus, and agree upon a "not to exceed" amount for the fee. And they will bring you the information.

Information brokers know which of the thousands of existing databases they should search to get you what you need. And they know the commands, the tricks and shortcuts, and the techniques needed to get the most out of an online system like Dialog, Nexis, Dow Jones News/Retrieval, Newsnet, and the rest. After all, this is what they do for a living.

We firmly believe that in years to come, executives, managers, and professionals will routinely use the services of their personal

information brokers the way they currently use accountants, C.P.A.s, doctors, dentists, and attorneys. Electronic information really is that important—and, frankly, that complex—that it requires the services of a professional.

The cheapest, easiest way to find such a professional is to ask your local librarians for recommendations. The vast majority of information brokers started out as librarians with M.L.S. (Master of Library Science) degrees. Alternatively, consider tracking down or buying *The Burwell Directory of Information Brokers*. It sells for about $85 and is simply *the* guide to the profession. For more information, contact:

Burwell Enterprises, Inc.
3724 F.M. 1960 West, Suite 214
Houston, TX 77068
(713) 537-8344
(713) 537-8332 (fax)
CompuServe: 75120,50

The matter of cost

The Internet, as we have seen, is an incredible resource. But the best thing and the worst thing about the Net is that it's *free!* Or if not absolutely free-of-charge, so cheap that it barely makes a difference.

On the one hand, it's great that masses of people have free or cheap access to the information and other resources the Net offers. But, on the other hand, there are no rewards for providing superb services and features, and no penalties for those who present shoddy, poorly managed features. When no one's paying and no one's being paid, no one cares.

In the commercial world, things are very, very different. Although the commercial online information industry is not without its problems, no one can deny that the quality, comprehensiveness, and currency of commercially-provided information is far superior to just about anything you will find on the Net. The profit motive, in effect, works wonders here as it does everywhere else.

Unfortunately, most commercial online information is grossly overpriced, in our opinion. A full discussion is not appropriate here, but the companies that prepare and provide commercial databases need to learn about *elasticity of demand*. If they lowered their prices, more people would use their services. After all, once information has been stored in digital form, the cost of delivering it to one person or a dozen is nearly the same. But the profit is almost 12 times greater.

Ours is not to reason why. But keeping these costs down is yet another reason for hiring a professional to do your searching for you.

The databases to search

According to the *Gale Directory of Databases*, the authoritative guide to the industry, there were 5,307 databases in 1994, available on a total of 812 systems. Just think of a system or online service as an "information department store" offering a selection of databases. (To give you an idea of the growth of this industry, in 1984, those numbers were 1,807 databases and 414 systems.)

Any one of those more than 5,000 databases could contain the information you need to "knock 'em dead" at your next job interview. If yours is a very highly focused interest, there is probably a database devoted to it. Again, this is where an information professional can help you.

A business sampler

If you intend to search on your own—or want to get a general idea of what's available from business-oriented databases—read on. We've picked out seven leading databases of business information for this sampler. Our thought was that these databases would be of greatest interest to the majority of readers.

But there are many other possibilities—such as searching a database containing back issues of the leading newspaper in a city or town.

Imagine this: You're set to fly out to interview with a company based in Akron, Ohio; or New Orleans, Louisiana; or St. Louis, Missouri. You grew up in Maine or Oregon or Florida, and you've never been to any of those cities. Yet you can easily arrange to search the *Akron Beacon Journal*, the *Times-Picayune*, or the *St. Louis Post-Dispatch*.

What was the name of the executive you are set to meet? Want to find out if he or she has been given any awards for community service in the last five years? Want to plug into the main issues and controversies in the town? And, by the way, has the firm made any major donations to the local hospital or other fund drives?

The answers to all of these questions—and much more information—can be found by doing a simple search of a database that includes the full text of the local paper. And such databases are *widely* available on systems like Dialog and DataTimes.

But now, to business. Once again, what you will find here is a mere *sampling* of business- and company-oriented databases. We make no pretense at being definitive. Our only goal is to alert you to the kinds of information and coverage you can expect to find among commercial online systems and databases.

✳ **American Business Directory**

Available via Dialog, this database covers 9.7 million companies (mainly privately held). It is based on the Yellow Pages annual reports as well as annual interviews. It includes estimates of sales, share of market, and other key items for most companies. You can search by ZIP code, city, county, state, area code, or metropolitan statistical area (MSA).

✳ **Company Intelligence**

Available via Data-Star/Dialog and Nexis, this database covers some 190,000 private and public companies. But the emphasis is on privately held firms. Also covered are nearly 30,000 international companies. The directory information comes from *Ward's Business Directory* and includes business descriptions and financials.

✳ Disclosure

This has long been the premier database of Securities and Exchange Commission (S.E.C.) company information—though the much anticipated, long-delayed EDGAR system has finally become available offering the same information from the U.S. government. (EDGAR is available on the Internet at the Gopher address **town.hall.org**.)

Disclosure offers information on 12,500 public companies in the U.S. with at least $5 million in assets. The information comes from S.E.C. filings and includes a description of the business, balance sheet, cash flow, income statement, financial ratios, president's letter, and management discussion.

This is a truly first-class database, and it is available via CompuServe, Data-Star/Dialog, Dow Jones, and Nexis.

✳ Dun's Market Identifiers USA

This database has over 7.6 million entries—public and private companies (mainly private), government agencies and contractors, and schools and universities. All have five or more employees or sales of over $1 million.

It's available via America Online, CompuServe, Data-Star/Dialog, Dow Jones, GEnie, Newsnet, and Prodigy. But the one thing you must always remember about Dun's and Dun & Bradsteet databases is that the information they offer is usually supplied by the companies themselves. No one goes into the field to investigate, verify, or otherwise collect information. At least not at this writing.

✳ Moody's Corporate Profiles

This database covers over 7,000 of the most important publicly held companies. It includes all New York and American Stock Exchange companies, plus 1,800 of the most active NASDAQ or over-the-counter companies. It provides business descriptions and financials. At this writing, Moody's is available via Dialog.

✳ **National College Databank (Peterson's Guides)**

There are actually two databases that cover the U.S. and Canada: Peterson's College Database contains about 3,450 post-secondary colleges/universities, while GRADLINE lists over 1,500 accredited institutions that award post-baccalaureate degrees.

Certainly this is useful for undergrads. But it is one of the main options for academic institution searching, at least in the non-Internet world. You will find Peterson's on CompuServe (College Database only), Dialog, and Dow Jones.

✳ **Standard & Poor's Corporate Descriptions Plus News**

This S&P database covers over 12,000 public companies, offering strategic and financial information and news. Records include business description, incorporation history, earnings and finances, capitalization summary, and stock and bond data. This S&P database can be found on Dialog, Dow Jones, Nexis, and Newsnet.

 # Conclusion

In the past decade or so, your co-authors have written many books about online databases and information retrieval. Clearly, this is not a subject that can be condensed into a single chapter of any book. But we can certainly give you the essence. We can certainly tell you what most people—most job-seeking people—need to know to put this incredible resource to work.

That's what we have tried to do here. It is only a slight exaggeration to say that today's online databases make it easy to find out anything about any person or company of interest. But *interest* is the key.

You can obtain and absorb an incredible amount of information about a company or industry using the tools we've identified here. But you are never going to fool anybody at a company into believing that you are a genuine expert. And, in any case, that should not be your goal.

 # Interest is the key

Your goal should be to demonstrate a genuine interest in the company, the industry, or the person doing the interviewing. And there is no better, more effective way to do this than to take the time—or spend the money—needed to bring yourself up to speed on the subjects at hand.

This has always been possible. Virtually all of the online databases that exist today started out as print publications, most of which are still available at a good library. But why spend hours—or days—doing by hand what you or your information broker can do in seconds using online databases?

That is very much the point of this chapter. We do not have space to tell you about all of the resources that exist. But we can definitely alert you to some of the possibilities and point you in the right direction.

 # What next?

There was a TV show in the early sixties that opened each episode with the line "There are a thousand stories in the naked city . . .." (Naturally, the show, a police drama, was called *Naked City*.) Well, there are a thousand *times* a thousand stories and needs of people looking for jobs.

It is our sincere hope that this book has helped. We have done our very best to locate, filter, and present you with the very best, most effective, tools. The emphasis has been on the Internet, of course. But we have not blindly limited you to Internet resources. Instead, we have shown you the realms of commercial systems like CompuServe and America Online, and peeped into "industrial-strength" systems like Dialog and Dow Jones. After all, once you have obtained the hardware and software needed to tap into the Net, you've automatically got just about everything you need to access any online system of any sort.

There's simply no doubt about it. In an increasingly technological economy, the best jobs are going to go to those who know how to use technology. And that's largely what we have tried to show you here—how to use the technology to get the job you want.

But be not afraid. As we hope we have shown, there is absolutely nothing magical about technology, however you may care to define it. Older people—which is to say, anyone above the age of 12—resist technology not because it is difficult, but because it is different from what they are comfortable with.

Do not be so constrained. You must chart your own course. But it is our fondest hope that you will enthusiastically grasp and use the tools we have presented in this book. Take the time—*make* the time—to get online with the Internet and possibly some commercial system. Do not be passive, but *engage* your mind and your personality.

Think. Ask questions. Take control of your destiny. Get in there and mix it up! Seize the power and go get the job you want! Strong words and a lot of exclamation points, but we all know you can do it. After all, you had the great good sense and wonderful perceptiveness to select and read this book. With your hard work, energy, and enthusiasm—and the information provided here—*you will succeed!*

Appendix

The Internet Toolkit
& Glossbrenner's
Choice

Computers, the Internet, and consumer online services aren't really all that difficult to use, provided you've got two things—the right information and the right software. We've done our best in this book to give you the right information. This appendix addresses the other need—the right software.

Through years of experience, your co-authors have become experts in public domain and shareware software for DOS/Windows machines. We know exactly what utilities and tools you need to make it easier than you've ever imagined to go online, and as a convenience to readers, we have long made them available on disk as part of a collection called Glossbrenner's Choice.

In addition to the software, however, Glossbrenner's Choice also offers a series of disks called the Internet Toolkit. These disks contain the FAQ (Frequently Asked Questions) files, the best guides to resources, and other information you'll need if you want to make the most of the Internet. With just two exceptions (Internet Disks 3 and 6), the disks in the Internet Toolkit contain plain, pure ASCII text files. Which means that they can be used by *both* DOS/Windows users and Macintosh users.

If you have a Macintosh . . .

The PowerPC chip notwithstanding, it is likely to be a while before Macintoshes and PCs can share the same software. But the two systems have long been able to share text files, thanks to Apple's SuperDrive 3.5-inch disk-drive technology. If your Mac was manufactured after August 1989, it is almost certainly equipped with one or more SuperDrives and thus has the ability to read 1.44MB Mac- and DOS-formatted disks.

Check your reference manual for an appendix titled "Exchanging Disks and Files with MS-DOS Computers," or words to that effect. As you will discover, the necessary Apple File Exchange software is supplied on one of the utility disks provided with your Mac system software. If you are using System 7.5, check your disks for a program called PC Exchange.

Follow the Apple File Exchange or PC Exchange instructions, and you will be able to copy the files on the Internet Toolkit disks onto your hard drive. Since the files are all plain ASCII text files, you can read and search them with your favorite word processor as easily as if you had created them yourself. There is no need to worry with any of the "translator" modules supplied with the Apple File Exchange software.

Glossbrenner's Choice disks

Here's a list of the disks described in this appendix:

The Internet Toolkit

Internet 1 Internet Must-Have Files
Internet 2 FTP Essentials
Internet 3 Telnet Essentials (DOS/Windows only)
Internet 4 Newsgroup Essentials
Internet 5 Mailing List Essentials
Internet 6 Compression and ConversionTools (DOS/Windows only)

Internet 7 Just the FAQs
Internet 8 World Wide Web Essentials
Internet 9 Making Money on the Internet Disk

DOS/Windows Tools & Utilities

Communicator's Toolchest
CommWin Communications Package
D-Lite for Delphi
Encryption Tools
Idea Processing
Instant File Management: QFILER, QEDIT, & Associates
Qmodem Communications Program
System Configuration Tools (Utilities 9)
TAPCIS for CompuServe
Text Search
Text Treaters

The Internet Toolkit

The disks in the Internet Toolkit collection contain key FAQs, directories, guides, lists, and other information about using various features of the Internet. Any word processing program can be used to view, print, and search the files for keywords.

All of the disks are 3.5-inch, high-density (1.44MB). Most computer users today have at least one drive in their systems that can read high-density disks. If you don't, you really should consider getting one. A high-density drive sells for about $40 at local computer stores. The only reason not to upgrade is if you've got a very old system that's not worth putting more money into. In which case, it's probably time to get a new computer.

Internet 1—Internet Must-Have Files (Mac-readable)

This disk includes the latest versions of the key text files which every Internet user should have—including the List of Subject-Oriented Internet Resource Guides you read about in Chapter 5. All of these

files are available on the Net, but you may want to avoid the hassle and get them in one neat package:

> ➤ *The Internet Services FAQ* by Kevin Savetz

> ➤ *Special Internet Connections* by Scott Yanoff

> ➤ *The Unofficial Internet Book List* by Kevin Savetz

> ➤ The List of Subject-Oriented Internet Resource Guides

> ➤ John December's *Internet-CMC List*

> ➤ John December's *Internet Tools Summary*

The disk also includes *The Beginner's Guide to the Internet*, an excellent tutorial for DOS and Windows users by Patrick J. Suarez.

✳ *The Internet Services FAQ*

Kevin Savetz is not only one of the most knowledgeable Internauts you are ever likely to find, he is also one of the best writers you are likely to encounter on the Net or in real life. His Frequently Asked Questions (FAQ) file on Internet basics is must reading for everyone. It includes sections like "I'm new to the Internet—Where do I start?", "What kind of information is on the Internet?", and "Are there any magazines about the Internet?"

Mr. Savetz has written a book based on his file. Look for *Your Internet Consultant: The FAQs of Life Online* by Kevin Savetz. Or call Sams Publishing at 800-428-5331 for more information.

✳ *Special Internet Connections*

This is the famous Yanoff List you are sure to hear about. It tells you about what Scott Yanoff feels are the best resources available on the Net for specific topics. Those topics range from Agriculture to Weather, Atmospheric, and Oceanic information. The Yanoff List calls on you to use all your fundamental Internet skills to get the information or goodies you want.

✳ *The Unofficial Internet Book List*

This is another super list prepared and maintained by Kevin Savetz. The reviews are only two or three sentences long, and Mr. Savetz makes no claim at comprehensiveness. (That's probably what the "Unofficial" is all about.) But in our opinion, he is right on target.

We were especially pleased to get a letter from Mr. Savetz after he read our *Internet Slick Tricks*. "I just wanted to let you know that I think it's great. I mean really great. I haven't seen a book this honest, readable, and fun since, well, mine :-) or *Internet Starter Kit for the Mac*. Congratulations on a fine job!"

✳ **The List of Subject-Oriented Internet Resource Guides**

Prepared by the Clearinghouse for Subject-Oriented Internet Resource Guides at the University of Michigan, this file is probably the single most important file for anyone who is truly interested in mining the deep information resources of the Net. The file itself is a directory—a list of *other* files and where to get them.

These other files have been prepared by professors and students and others, and each one pulls together and presents in one neat package information on the main resources available via the Internet on a particular subject. For more on the Clearinghouse, see Chapter 5.

✳ **John December's** *Internet-CMC List*

The full title of this incredible resource is *Information Sources: The Internet and Computer-Mediated Communication* by John December. This list is essentially a wonderfully detailed table. It organizes and categorizes resources by topic and gives you the Internet feature to use (FTP, Gopher, etc.), the address to target, and the path to follow once you get there.

There are so many wonderful things to say about Mr. December's continually updated publication that, instead of saying anything, we will say the one thing that matters: Get the list!

✳ **John December's *Internet Tools Summary***

Ditto for this John December file as well. Among the Internet Information Retrieval Tools this file discusses are Finger, Netfind, Nslookup, Ping, WHOIS, X.500, Archie, FTP, Jughead, Knowbot, Maltshop, Trickle, and Veronica.

In each case, Mr. December gives you a quick handle on the tool and then tells you where to get more information on how to use it, tips, demos, and so on. As a word of caution: You must have some idea of what Telnet and FTP mean and how to use these features to be able to understand and benefit from either December list. (See Internet 2 for Telnet information and Internet 3 for FTP information.)

 # Internet 2—FTP Essentials (Mac-readable)

As you know from Chapter 3, FTP stands for "File Transfer Protocol." Although not absolutely essential for taking advantage of the Internet's job-related features, FTP is an important Internet skill for anyone who wants to tap the Net's in-depth information and shareware software resources. You will find a complete, Glossbrenner-written, step-by-step tutorial for using FTP on this disk.

In addition, you will find an excellent FAQ by Perry Rovers on the subject, including a list of FTP sites that's about as comprehensive as one can imagine.

 # Internet 3—Telnet Essentials

For DOS and Windows users only, this disk contains Peter Scott's remarkable Hytelnet package. The package includes a gigantic database of Telnet locations, with at least one screen per location describing what you'll find there. It is, in effect, a gigantic, computerized directory of Telnet sites.

For ease of use, the entire thing is organized as a hypertext-style menu system. Also on this disk is Bruce Clouette's optional Subject

Guide for the main Hytelnet menu, as well as a Windows front-end program, WINHytelnet.

Internet 4—Newsgroup Essentials (Mac-readable)

Internet newsgroups are important sources of information. But as you know from Chapter 16, they are also the ideal place to make contacts and establish relationships that could lead to job opportunities. On this disk you'll find two lists of Internet newsgroups—organized by newsgroup category (alternative, computer, recreation, science, etc.). The best way to use these files is to put them on your hard disk and then bring them into your word processing program, where you can use a "search" feature to locate keywords on the lists.

We've also included the DOS program ROT13.EXE, a utility you can use to encode and decode off-color jokes and the like found in some of the humor-oriented groups.

And should you want to create your own newsgroup, you will find two valuable information files on this disk. One outlines the procedure for creating an ALT newsgroup; the other does the same for the other kinds of newsgroups.

Internet 5—Mailing List Essentials (Mac-readable)

This disk contains two gigantic lists of Internet and Bitnet mailing list: The SRI List of Lists and Publicly Accessible Mailing Lists (PAML). Nearly every existing mailing list gets a meaty paragraph-long write-up, usually prepared by the list's creator. These write-ups offer lots of keywords for you to find when you bring the following files into your word processing program and apply its "search" function:

 # Internet 6—Compression and Conversion Tools

This disk is for DOS and Windows users only. It contains all of the programs you will need to uncompress or unarchive or decode the various files you will find at FTP sites around the Net. File compression and archiving (bundling several files into a single file for easier downloading) have long been popular in the world of commercial online systems and bulletin boards. And fortunately, only a few main techniques and formats are used, principally ZIP and ARC in the DOS/Windows worlds and StuffIt in the Mac world.

Unfortunately, this kind of simplicity does not rule on the Net. Over the years Net users have developed any number of ways to compress and/or archive files. If you want to be able to uncompress and unarchive those files, you've got to have the correct utility program. That's what this disk provides. Among many others, it gives you the programs you need to deal with files that end in .ARC, .ARJ, .BTOA, .CPIO, .GZ or .Z, .HQX, .SIT, .TAR, .UUE, .Z, and more.

 # Internet 7—Just the FAQs (Mac-readable)

On this disk you will find two things. First, there is the gigantic 100-plus page FAQ Index listing all of the FAQ files currently available on the Internet. The FAQ Index includes precise filenames to help you locate the files via Archie. Once you know where a file lives, you can log onto that site and get a copy via anonymous FTP.

Second, there are what we feel are some of the key FAQ files you may want to have on hand (in addition to the ones already described.) Here's just a sampling:

➤ Addresses FAQ—How to find e-mail addresses and locate people on the Internet.

➤ Compression FAQ—All about compression programs. Where to find them, how to use them, troubleshooting, and more.

> Gopher FAQ—Questions and answers about using Internet Gophers.

> Pictures FAQ—Information on graphics images on the Internet, newsgroups devoted to graphics, decoding and encoding images, image formats, and so forth.

> Veronica FAQ—Answers to frequently asked questions about using the Veronica search utility on the Internet.

⇨ Internet 8—World Wide Web Essentials (Mac-readable)

This disk contains a huge amount of information about the World Wide Web, including:

> *Entering the World Wide Web: A Guide to Cyberspace* by Kevin Hughes

> *A Beginner's Guide to HTML* from the National Center for Supercomputing Applications (NCSA)

> *A Beginner's Guide to URLs* from NCSA

> *The URL FAQ* by Alan Coopersmith

> *The List of WWW Service Providers* by Mary E. S. Morris

> *Interesting Business Sites on the Web* by Bob O'Keefe

> *The World Wide Web FAQ* by Thomas Boutell

Some of the files on this disk are in HTML format. These are plain text files, so anyone can read them. But they contain hypertext markup language text codes that make it possible for you to read the files with Mosaic or Netscape Navigator, or some other Web browser. Or you can use the DOS program DE-HTML.EXE supplied on the disk to strip the HTML coding from these (or any other) HTML files.

Internet 9—Making Money on the Internet (Mac-readable)

This disk contains lots of really great stuff for anyone who wants to know more about selling products and services on the Internet. We assembled it when we were researching and writing another book, *Making Money on the Internet*. Among the text files you'll find on this disk are:

> ➤ *Advertising on the Internet FAQ* by Michael Strangelove
>
> ➤ *International Connectivity* by Larry Landweber
>
> ➤ *FAQ: International E-mail Accessibility* by Olivier M.J. Crepin-Leblond
>
> ➤ *The Internet Mall* by Dave Taylor (excerpts)
>
> ➤ *The Internet Press: A Guide to Electronic Journals about the Internet* by Kevin Savetz
>
> ➤ *Internet Pearls* by William Hogg of SoloTech Software
>
> ➤ *The POCIA List* (Providers of Commercial Internet Access) by Celestin Company
>
> ➤ *Guide to Network Resource Tools* by EARN Associates
>
> ➤ *A Primer on How to Work with the Usenet Community* by Chuq Von Rospach

Also on this disk, for DOS/Windows users, is a program called Internet Acronyms from William Hogg's SoloTech software. Searchable, viewable, printable, or accessible as a TSR, Internet Acronyms gives you close to 200 pages of Net acronyms and file extensions and their meanings. DOS and Windows users will also find a program called NetDemo from Rick Hower that serves as an interactive tutorial for using many of the Internet's main features.

Sure, it's "retro" of us to say so in an age when everything is supposed to be "on the Net," but when you think about the tons of information that can be delivered for $5 on a 3.5-inch disk, compared to the amount of time and money you would have to spend to locate, download, and decompress the same files, opting for the on-disk solution makes a lot of sense.

DOS/Windows tools and utilities

It's been our experience over the years that, whatever computing task you want to accomplish, there's almost always a program that can easily do it. In fact, there are often several programs that fill the bill. The trick is to *find* the programs and pick the very best ones. That's what our Glossbrenner's Choice collection of software for DOS/Windows users is all about.

All of the programs are fully functional, and most are extensively documented in ready-to-print manuals. The software itself is either *public domain* (PD) or *shareware*. Public domain programs are yours to do with as you please. But if you like and regularly use a *shareware* program, you are honor-bound to send the programmer the requested registration fee, typically $15 to $25. No one can force you to do this, of course. But when you see a really good piece of software, supporting its creator's efforts is something you will sincerely want to do.

Communicator's Toolchest

If the comm program you use doesn't have the ZMODEM protocol, you can use the tools provided on this disk to add it. ZMODEM is quite simply the best download protocol, and every online communicator should have access to it.

The disk also includes a program for adding support for CompuServe's QB (Quick B) protocol to virtually any comm program. This is by far the best protocol to use when you are downloading files from the data libraries of CompuServe's forums. Like ZMODEM, this protocol has the ability to resume an interrupted download at a later time. Just sign on and start the download again, and it will pick up right where it left off.

The disk also contains several other extremely useful utility programs to make life online easier.

CommWin Communications Program

Our current favorite comm program for Windows users is Gerard E. Bernor's CommWin program. It's quick, clean, intuitive, and beats the Windows terminal program all hollow.

D-Lite for Delphi

If you regularly use Delphi mail and SIGs, this DOS program can save you money. D-Lite lets you do all of your thought work offline, signing on only to pick up messages, mail, and files, or to blast them into the system. It's really a must for any heavy Delphi user.

Encryption Tools

You have to assume that if your e-mail *can* be read it *will* be. Thus, it is always a good idea to encrypt sensitive information before sending it electronically. The programs on this disk can so thoroughly encrypt a binary or text file that cipher experts from the National Security Agency or CIA would have a tough time decoding the results. If you have the key, however, you can decrypt files in an instant.

Among other things, this disk includes Philip Zimmermann's famous *Pretty Good Privacy* (PGP) public key RSA encryption program. For more on Mr. Zimmermann, see the Steven Levy cover story "The Cypherpunks vs. Uncle Sam" in the June 12, 1994, issue of the *New York Times Sunday Magazine*.

Idea Processing

PC-Outline is an incredible clone of the commercial idea outlining program, Thinktank. Indeed, many former Thinktank users prefer this shareware product. PC-Outline lets you randomly enter information of almost any type (thoughts, plans, ideas, etc.) and then organize it into a hierarchical structure.

You can then go from viewing the lowest level of detail to a view that shows you only the highest, most important topics. You can also print the outline, copy it into another outline, or paste it directly into your word processor. Ideal for organizing projects, reports, books, and lists—or just organizing your thoughts!

 # Instant File Management: QFILER, QEDIT, & Associates

QFILER (Quick Filer) by Kenn Flee gives you *complete* control over your files and disk directories. You can tag a group of dissimilar files for deletion or for copying to another disk or directory. You can easily move up and down your directory trees, altering the date and time stamps of files, changing their attributes, compressing, uncompressing, and peering into archives. You can also look at any file on the screen, copy it to your printer, and more. You will find QFILER much easier to use than the Windows 3.1 File Manager or similar DOS-based products.

Also on this disk is WHEREIS, a lightning fast Archie-like file finder. And QEDIT, the famous DOS text-editing program. QEDIT specializes in creating plain text of the sort you must use on the Internet and in most e-mail letters on other systems. Yet it gives you many of the convenience features of a full-blown word processor.

 # Qmodem Communications Program

Here's what a recent issue of *Computer Shopper* had to say about Qmodem from Mustang Software: "This is simply the best DOS-based shareware communications package you can find . . . simple to set up and use, and it features about *every* bell and whistle you expect from a communications package . . . a true powerhouse . . ."

269

The article goes on to note that Qmodem "bears a great deal of similarity to the ever-popular shareware program Procomm, right down to the key commands . . . This shareware program is superior to the shareware version of Procomm, however, because when Procomm went commercial, Datastorm stopped developing the shareware version. Mustang, on the other hand, has continually updated the free version of Qmodem, and will continue to do so. It's hard to beat the power, and you can't beat the price."

We heartily agree. If you don't have a first-class comm program yet, try Qmodem.

System Configuration Tools (Utilities 9)

This disk includes the UARTTOOLS program (UARTID.EXE) discussed in Chapter 1. This program allows you to find out whether any of your COM ports have the 16550A National Semiconductor UART, and if so, what interrupts they are using. Also on the disk are such intriguing DOS tools as BAT2EXEC (converts a batch program to an .EXE file), PopDOS (lets you shell out to DOS from any program), and UMBFILES (a hands-on memory management tool).

TAPCIS for CompuServe

TAPCIS makes it easy to handle electronic mail and get the most out of CompuServe forums. It will automatically sign on, pick up your e-mail, and check forums you have specified for messages addressed to you. Then you can sign off, review the information TAPCIS has gathered, and draft replies using the built-in editor. TAPCIS will then sign on again and automatically upload your e-mail and forum message replies. The whole idea is to make using CompuServe as easy and inexpensive as possible.

TAPCIS can do the same thing when it comes to uploading and downloading files. Just tell it what to do offline, then stand back and let it sign on and zip around the system.

 # Text Search

This disk contains the programs AnyWord, LOOKFOR, and FGREP. AnyWord by Eric Balkan can parse any text file, build its own index of keywords, and make it easy to search the file using sophisticated search logic. LOOKFOR works even faster. It lets you do AND, OR, wildcard, and proximity searches of text files—with no prior indexing. You can then print (to disk or printer) relevant file excerpts. FGREP by Chris Dunford operates in a similar way, though it is more UNIX-like and not quite so user-friendly.

 # Text Treaters

This disk contains some 45 programs to manipulate, filter, and prepare a text file in virtually any way you can imagine. These programs are particularly convenient when you're dealing with text you get from e-mail correspondents and Internet sites.

For example, a program called TEXT lets you remove all leading white space on each line of a file, remove all trailing blanks, or convert all white space into the number of spaces you specify. CHOP will cut a file into the number of pieces you specify. CRLF makes sure that every line in a text file ends with a carriage return and a linefeed so it can be displayed and edited properly. There's also a package by Peter Norton to create an index for a report, document, book, or whatever.

 # Order Form

You can use the order form on the next page (or a photocopy) to order Glossbrenner's Choice disks. Or you may simply write your request on a piece of paper and send it to us. Disks are $5 each, plus $3 for shipping to U.S. addresses ($5 outside the U.S.).

We accept Visa and MasterCard, as well as checks or money orders made payable to Glossbrenner's Choice. (U.S. funds drawn on a U.S.

bank or international money orders only.) Please allow one to two weeks for delivery. For additional information, please write or call:

Glossbrenner's Choice
699 River Road
Yardley, PA 19067-1965
Voice: 215-736-1213
Fax: 215-736-1031
E-mail: Alfred@Delphi.com

Glossbrenner's Choice Order Form for Readers of *Finding a Job on the Internet*

Name_____

Address_____

City_____State_____ZIP_____

Province/Country_____Phone_____

Payment [ ] Check or Money Order payable to **Glossbrenner's Choice**

       [ ] Visa/MC_____Exp___/___

Signature_____

Send to: Glossbrenner's Choice   Voice: 215-736-1213
          699 River Road   Fax: 215-736-1031
          Yardley, PA 19067-1965   E-mail: Alfred@Delphi.com

The Internet Toolkit
____Internet 1 Internet Must-Have Files
____Internet 2 FTP Essentials
____Internet 3 Telnet Essentials
____Internet 4 Newsgroup Essentials
____Internet 5 Mailing List Essentials
____Internet 6 Compression and Conversion Tools
____Internet 7 Just the FAQs
____Internet 8 World Wide Web Essentials
____Internet 9 Making Money on the Internet

Other Glossbrenner's Choice Disks
____Communicator's Toolchest
____CommWin Communications Program
____D-Lite for Delphi
____Encryption Tools
____Idea Processing
____Instant File Management: QFILER, QEDIT, & Associates
____Qmodem Communications Program
____System Configuration Tools (Utilities 9)
____TAPCIS for CompuServe
____Text Search
____Text Treaters

____Total number of disks, 3.5-inch HD ($5 per disk)   _____

Glossbrenner Books (Book prices include $3 for Book Rate shipping.)
____*The Little Online Book* ($21)   _____
____*Making Money on the Internet* ($23)   _____
____*Internet 101: A College Student's Guide* ($23)   _____
____*Internet Slick Tricks* ($19)   _____
____*The Information Broker's Handbook* ($38)   _____

                            TOTAL   _____

Pennsylvania residents, please add 6% Sales Tax.   _____

Shipping Charge ($3.00 for shipment to U.S. addresses
   and $5.00 for shipment outside the U.S.)   _____

            GRAND TOTAL ENCLOSED   _____

Index

Illustrations are in **boldface**.

About the authors

Alfred Glossbrenner is the author of more than 30 books on the Internet, online services, and other topics. Hailed as "The Great Communicator" by the *New York Times*, he has also written extensively about careers and job-search techniques. His credits in that area include recruitment brochures for the Sun Oil Company and award-winning career-oriented filmstrips for the Changing Times Education Service. He was also a contributing author to Baker & Taylor's 12-volume *Career Information Center* and has served as a consultant and writer for the Center for Occupational and Professional Assessment at Educational Testing Service (ETS).

Emily Glossbrenner has nearly two decades' experience in computing, marketing, and career services, including nine years with the IBM Corporation and six years with Educational Testing Service. While at ETS, she served on the project team for the System of Interactive Guidance and Information (SIGI), the first computer-based system designed to help college students make career decisions. She is the co-author of *Internet Slick Tricks* and *Making Money on the Internet*, and has contributed to numerous books and articles about the Internet, online services, and other aspects of personal computing.

The Glossbrenners live in a 1790s farmhouse on the Delaware River in Bucks County, Pennsylvania.